TELL THOSE WHO MOURN

There Is a Way through the Darkness of Grief

SHARON M. CAPRA

WESTBOW
PRESS®
A DIVISION OF THOMAS NELSON
& ZONDERVAN

This book is a work of non-fiction. Unless otherwise noted, the author and the publisher make no explicit guarantees as to the accuracy of the information contained in this book and in some cases, names of people and places have been altered to protect their privacy.

Scripture quotations taken from the New American Standard Bible®, Copyright © 1960, 1962, 1963, 1968, 1971, 1972, 1973, 1975, 1977, 1995 by The Lockman Foundation. Used by permission. (www.Lockman.org)

Scripture taken from the New King James Version. Copyright © 1979, 1980, 1982 by Thomas Nelson, Inc. Used by permission. All rights reserved.

Author photo by Nathan Lee

WestBow Press books may be ordered through booksellers or by contacting:

WestBow Press
A Division of Thomas Nelson & Zondervan
1663 Liberty Drive
Bloomington, IN 47403
www.westbowpress.com
1 (866) 928-1240

Because of the dynamic nature of the Internet, any web addresses or links contained in this book may have changed since publication and may no longer be valid. The views expressed in this work are solely those of the author and do not necessarily reflect the views of the publisher, and the publisher hereby disclaims any responsibility for them.

Any people depicted in stock imagery provided by Thinkstock are models, and such images are being used for illustrative purposes only. Certain stock imagery © Thinkstock.

ISBN: 978-1-5127-0931-5 (sc)
ISBN: 978-1-5127-0932-2 (hc)
ISBN: 978-1-5127-0930-8 (e)

Library of Congress Control Number: 2015913580

Print information available on the last page.

WestBow Press rev. date: 09/28/2015

CONTENTS

ACKNOWLEDGMENTS

I am so thankful for my husband, Tony. We've been so blessed in our marriage, our family, and in all our adventures together. I love you very much.

For each of my twelve children who have inspired me to go beyond my limitations and strive for what God has called me for.

> Tony, a man who was willing to lay down his life for his family, friends, and country.
>
> Jason, a man of compassion who's always willing to help those around him.
>
> James, a strong leader who is generous with his life.
>
> Mike, a mighty warrior who doesn't back down in the face of fear.
>
> Rachel, a woman who praises God from the depths of her heart.
>
> Sarah, a woman who touches God through her worship.
>
> Joseph, a teacher of His Word who's filled with the courage to live a life of faith.
>
> Jacob, a God magnet who draws people to our Father's goodness.
>
> Danielle, a woman of grace who's filled with a deep commitment to the One she loves.

Joanna, a mighty warrior of God whose life is filled with great adventures in Christ.
Julia, a woman who has the humble heart of a servant willing to love even when it's hard.
Emily, a leader for Christ who appreciates the lives God has placed in her path.

Foremost, I thank my Deliverer, Jesus, who walked with me, cried with me, and held me while I went through pain. He is amazing!

Jesus knows that my son, Tony, is in heaven enjoying all the blessings there. He came and sat with a mom who was desperately sad. At my lowest emotional state, He lifted me up to see the deliverance He provided. I am so grateful.

F O R E W O R D

Tell Those Who Mourn: A Clinic

A common indictment of contemporary Christianity is that it's superficial and shallow, lacking in the ability to develop depth of character and moral fortitude among believers. This book is a sound repudiation of that indictment. In *Tell Those Who Mourn*, Sharon Capra opens her soul and brings the reader on a harrowing emotional and spiritual journey into every parent's worst nightmare. She describes how God informs, accompanies, comforts, and guides us through the depths of grief and, in time, back to the land of the living.

Nothing about this book is shallow or superficial. It's real, raw, and filled with unrelenting, dogged faith in Jesus Christ and God's unchanging Word. It's a true story of brokenness and grief, but it is also a story of victory.

In sports, a player or team demonstrating exemplary performance in a game or tournament is said to be "putting on a clinic." Sharon puts on a clinic of faith in this book, illuminating through her pain and grief a pure pathway of righteousness in the face of unspeakable tragedy.

The reward received is apparent in the godly wisdom that shines through Sharon's testimony, poetry, and biblical insight. In addition, the sections her husband and children wrote reveal the power of Jesus to meet us all where we are, strengthen the family, and bring comfort and restoration to all.

This book is an invaluable teaching tool and an amazing gift to the body of Christ. Through Sharon's strong-willed determination to break toward God in her grief, we more fully apprehend the words of St. Paul, "I can do all things through Christ who strengthens me."

—Robert A. Engelhardt
Pastor, Author, Speaker

INTRODUCTION

The title *Tell Those Who Mourn* came from Isaiah 61:3: "To proclaim the acceptable year of the LORD, and the day of vengeance of our God, to comfort all who mourn, to console those who mourn in Zion, to give them beauty for ashes, the oil of joy for mourning." Please note that the biblical citations used in this book come from the New King James version unless otherwise noted.

When my oldest son, Tony, was killed, I desperately needed God. I felt lost. I was in uncharted territory and needed guidance from my Lord. As you read this book, you will encounter several truths from God and His Word that I found on my days of mourning.

Throughout this book, you will also read the testimonies of others who have lived through the crushing reality of losing loved ones. You will witness how they handled their grief and how they found Christ's everlasting victory during their hardest trials.

My prayer is that this book will be a blessing and a help to everyone who reads it. This book doesn't offer the perfect formula for getting through a loved one's death, but it does allow readers to observe someone living with such a loss while clinging desperately to the Father.

Death can make us feel so hopeless. Some of us on this journey may require professional help, and I encourage them to seek the help they need. But the Word of God clearly states that death no longer has the sting of finality and that the grave doesn't have any victory; we, God's children, have His victory because we have eternal life through His Son. Death is but a temporary separation between us and those who have gone on before us.

In 1 Corinthians 15:55 (NIV) we read, "Where, O death, is your victory? Where, O death, is your sting?" God cares. He hears our cries. He provides help through His Son. Jesus bore our grief and carried our sorrows so believers could be free from the deep, hopeless anguish that grief brings. When such strong, negative emotions try to occupy our thoughts, we can proclaim with confidence that we are free from hopeless sorrow because of what Jesus did for us. However, we cannot avoid the pain of missing a loved one; that is a very human response we will experience on earth.

Isaiah 53:4 tells us, "Surely he hath borne our griefs and carried our sorrows." If you are going through a loss, I pray you will allow God's Spirit to comfort and encourage you. Please seek God with your whole heart, soul, and mind as you walk this journey. He is not only able to help you, He is also ready and willing to do that for you.

> Blessed be the God and Father of our Lord Jesus Christ, the Father of mercies, and God of all comfort; who comforts us in all our tribulation. (2 Corinthians 1:3–4)

Caught by Surprise

Waking up to the sounds of the upcoming spring day is such a terrific way to rise out of slumber. I hear birds calling to each other, and the sun is shining warmly through my bedroom window. Seven of my children are still sleeping, so I have some quiet time before they wake up. I look at my husband, who is sleeping soundly. It's rare to find him still in bed on a Wednesday morning. After serving over twenty five years in the Air Force, he retired and found employment in Washington, DC. He typically leaves for work by 6:00 a.m. every day.

I have so much to do today. I have homeschooled our twelve children for the past eighteen years, and even though five of the twelve have graduated from high school, every day is still filled with school, home, or church. I force myself to get up for my morning prayer time before everyone else wakes up.

I walk out of my bedroom and contemplate what I should do first. Determined to begin each day by praying for my family, I sit in our sunroom and open my Bible. My mind immediately drifts to the women's Bible study I'm leading and all the homework I still have to complete. I force myself to focus and remind myself to pray for my son Tony. Tony, the oldest son of our twelve children, is in Iraq on his fourth deployment. He entered the Air Force with a clear conviction it was what he wanted to do with his life, but of course having a father who had been in the Air Force might have contributed to his desire.

After basic training, he went to a military training school to learn how to be an explosive ordinance disposal (EOD) technician. Since 9/11, EOD technicians have had a critical role in protecting Americans from terrorism at home and abroad. They have helped save countless lives by searching for bombs and deactivating them. His was (and still is) a tough and rigorous program, yet he persevered and graduated. Tony told us he found his role so rewarding. As I pray for him, I'm not worried; I'm confident nothing will happen to him. I pray every morning for his safety. I remind myself it's so good to have this kind of confidence in God.

Everyone starts to rise, and I reluctantly get off the couch and start breakfast. I remember that my husband hasn't left for work. I run into the bedroom to see why he hasn't gotten up. He informs me he isn't going to the office today. That's the most bizarre response I've ever heard from him regarding work. He always goes to work whether he wants to or not. Even when he had severe back issues while in the military, he would still roll out of bed. Sometimes, he would have to lie down on the floor a couple of times, but he'd eventually make his way out of the house and to work. When he had a toothache, he would go to work. When he had a bad headache, he would go to work. Not once have I ever heard him say he just didn't feel like going in to work. Puzzled, I leave the room and ponder many times during the morning what he said.

The sounds of controlled chaos start to rise out of every room of the house as the kids look for their schoolbooks, eat breakfast, get dressed, and pick on their siblings. We all go down to the sunroom for the typical Mom-led Bible devotion time. I pick a verse, and we discuss it—or should I say *I* discuss it.

I spot two kids on the couch fighting over a blanket they both claim. A dog jumps up on the couch, and Jake squeals in his familiar, high-pitched voice when he calls the dog's name. Sarah is in the rocking chair reading her latest book. The other kids are barely listening. I ask myself, *Why am I doing this?* I proceed regardless of their lack of interest because I have a mission, and it includes finishing up this devotion and starting homeschool for the day.

Danielle, my fifteen-year-old, asks if her friend Rachel can come over after lunch. I agree and use her friend's impending visit to motivate Danielle to finish her schoolwork.

The kids begin school reluctantly, and we struggle slowly through the morning. Around ten, I head to the bedroom to check on my husband. He's wide awake, but he still isn't getting ready. I question him again as to why he doesn't want to go to work. He becomes annoyed, but he gives me the same response as earlier. I get angry with him for changing our routine. I leave the bedroom because I have more important issues to deal with.

Finally, lunchtime arrives, and we all pour into the kitchen. The refrigerator door opens and closes as hands reach in to grab meats, cheeses, and other edibles. The counters in the kitchen fill up with food. Sarah makes her typical Ramen noodle soup and heads out with Danielle to pick up her friend Rachel. I begin quickly straightening the house because I don't want Danielle's friend thinking we're a messy, unorganized family!

It is a beautiful April day. We live in northern Virginia, so our cold winters make gorgeous spring days a welcome sight. Some of the kids run to the trampoline and scream and laugh as usual as they pile in and start jumping.

Emily and Julia, the youngest Capras, are desperately trying to get their turns on the trampoline, and a minor argument erupts. Finally, Sarah defends them, they get on, and the laughing continues. I love the sounds of our children having a good time. What a perfect day of sunshine and smiling!

But I'm resolved to get back to work. I grab my lunch and head to the apartment we have behind our three-car garage. It's a total mess. Thankfully, I have this place to keep my school supplies, books, pencils, erasers, notebooks, and the other such tools for homeschooling. Assorted school papers cover the floor, counters, and table. I slowly start to clean up but decide to look at the women's Bible study notebook I happen to spot amid all the mess. The new lesson that I open to has a verse. I try to memorize the verse, but I struggle remembering it: "For the mountains shall depart and the hills be removed, but My kindness shall not depart from you, nor shall My covenant of peace be removed says the LORD who has mercy on you" (Isaiah 54:10).

Come on, Sharon! This verse isn't that hard to memorize! I tell myself. As I give thought to the words, I think about how amazing His Word is. No matter what uncertain events we experience, His love and peace are our constants. Praise God!

My meditation is interrupted as the door to the apartment opens and closes as kids and dogs run in and out. Joanna comes running into the room laughing. I ask her to clean up the apartment. I want to memorize the verse.

Danielle comes into the apartment and walks to where I'm sitting. She says Dad wants me. I'm annoyed because I'm trying to memorize my verse and don't want to go and see what he wants. "Do you know what he wants?" I ask.

"I don't know," she says. "Some policemen are here. Dad wants you."

I rise and walk to the back deck, where I see my husband standing. I smile at him, but he doesn't smile back. He has a strange, serious look. I'm confused. I ask him if he's all right. He doesn't reply. He walks back to the door to the house. *This is very strange.* I follow him. I assume the police are there to ask for a donation. We've had folks from many groups come to our house for that reason. I ask my husband what they want, but he asks me to stay outside. He says he'll be right back.

I stand there for a second. I'm puzzled. I make my way up the back deck to enter the French doors leading to the kitchen. I see my husband leading three Air Force personnel toward me on the deck. My husband passes me. I ask, "Why are they here? Why are they here?" He says in a voice too quiet for me to hear, "They're here for only one reason."

We all go out the door and stand on the deck. The children, who are in the house, are looking through the French doors watching us. My husband listens to them. I'm standing outside their circle. At that second, a bizarre thing happens to me. I look at the four of them talking and tell myself, *They shouldn't be here. They don't belong here.*

I am aware of what is about to unfold, but I try as hard as I can to deny the reality of the situation. This is the death notification team; they usually come in a group of two or three. We have at our house the notification officer, a chaplain, and a nurse. Sometimes, the team might also bring an officer who waits in the car in case the person receiving the notification gets violent.

The notification team is in their class-A uniforms. They have come with the worst of news and try to deliver the message with care and compassion. Everything is surreal. My heart is pounding so loudly that I can barely hear what they're talking about. I cover my ears. I hear myself saying, "No, No, No!"

The notification team looks at my husband and then at me. I heard, "Mr. and Mrs. Capra, I regret to inform you—"

Time slows down. I stop repeating, "No, No, No!" I have to listen to what they are trying to say. It is horrible. Time stands still. My four oldest sons—Tony, Jason, James, and Michael—are all in the Air Force. I don't know which one's name they will finish the sentence with.

Then I heard my firstborn son's name.

"Technical Sergeant Anthony Capra died in action at Golden Hills in Iraq."

I drop to my knees. I fall to the ground. I can't move. I can't think. I can't live. I can't breathe. I can't understand this. *This cannot be. No. Something is wrong here. God is protecting him. He couldn't have been killed. No. Something's totally wrong.* I hear my husband asking questions that make no sense to me. *How can he be so calm and logical at a time like this? Why isn't he turning inside out like me?*

The chaplain stoops beside me. He is very kind. He tries to help me up, but I refuse to move. The whole world is moving, just like when you've been on a boat for a while and just get off. Time stops. The chaplain asks me if he can do something for me or call anyone. I ask him to call our church and let our pastor know. I'm not aware of my children watching us from inside the house.

I suddenly remember Tony's wife, Angie, and their five children. I reach out for my husband's hand. "Tony, what about Angie? What about his children?" He looks at me and then at the notification team. In a very concerned voice, he asks, "Does Angie know?" They say a notification team is telling her at the same time we are finding out.

I remember when Tony met Angie. Five months prior to their meeting, we'd been assigned to Incirlik Air Base in Turkey. Typically, base housing is meant for smaller families, but we were a family of almost twelve tightly packed into a thousand-square-foot home. Living on a military base is like living in a small town—you get to know your neighbors. As a family, we had moved over seventeen times; we'd lived in Greece, Turkey, and South Korea, so we were accustomed to that type of living. Many families lived near us on base. During the afternoons, we could hear children of all ages, teens, and adults enjoying each other's company. Our older boys always found activities to do outside our cramped living quarters.

Tony met Angie at the NCO club on Incirlik Air Base. Angie's mom was an Air Force Staff Sergeant who had been stationed in Turkey. I remember Tony telling me about Angie. I was in the final phases of labor with my daughter, Joanna, when my then-eighteen-year-old son burst into the labor and delivery area. "Mom, Mom! I met the most amazing, beautiful woman!" Through my pants and groans, I said, "That's nice, Tony."

After the birth and happy moments, I sat up in bed with my sweet baby girl in my arms and thought about how Angie might be my future daughter-in-law. I smiled as I thought about how I'd just had a baby and could be marrying off my oldest.

They fell in love very quickly and were engaged soon after. We had a beautiful backyard wedding, filled with all kinds of Italian and Turkish food. We invited all our friends and neighbors.

Once they married, they were no longer military dependents and had to go back to the States. They moved in with my husband's brother, Doug, and soon afterward, Tony joined the Air Force.

I remember the news we had just heard, and I am propelled back to the reality of the moment. I have to see Angie. I have no idea how we will all understand this. My heart aches beyond belief.

The death notification team leaves. My husband opens the door to the back deck, and all the kids pour outside. Joe, his fiancée Dillon, Jake, Danielle, Joanna, Julia, and Emily gather, and my husband says a prayer. He begins talking to our children. I look around at them. Some are hugging each other, some are sitting on the bench with their heads down, and others are covering their faces and crying.

I run inside. I have nowhere to hide. I'm trying to find refuge. I remember being five and hearing my mom calling me to go to the doctor's for a vaccination. I hid in my brothers' closet under the hanging clothes so no one could find me. It was dark. I felt safe until my mother found me. I find myself desiring to go back to that closet in my thoughts and hide. I flee to my bedroom, fall on my bed, and cry.

I yearn to hear my mother and father's voices. My mom is dealing with Alzheimer's and cannot talk to me anymore. She was diagnosed over ten years ago; her progression with Alzheimer's has been very slow. In the beginning, she would forget just everyday events or where she had put something. But now, she can no longer remember my family and barely remembers my name. She would be such a comfort to me right now. I reach for the phone to call my dad. My dad and my brother, Paul, have been taking care of my mom so she could live at home. I can barely dial. My hands are trembling.

He picks up the phone. I cry out, "Dad, Tony has been killed! Dad, my baby is dead!" My father makes a guttural groan. "Oh no! Oh no!" He relays the message to Paul. We can say no more.

After I hang up, I tell my husband we have to see Angie. We hug, and I sob. This is unbelievable. How could this have happened?

A Place

There is a sad place on earth
Where we are sometimes forced to walk
It is not wide
And firm beneath our feet
We feel unable
To go forward or backward
No one can take
Our place
All our senses
Are heightened
And keep us in this
Uncomfortable place
It's like a dream
You wish to wake
Up from but cannot
I cry to the Lord
But get no response
I know that You hear me
O Lord and my Father
Come to me
And lift me away from here
I know that you are able
And You hear me
All I know to do
Is seek You and believe

You will take care of me
In this horrible place
That I am in

—Sharon Capra

We tell the kids we're going to see Angie. She lives a little over an hour and a half away, so I want to pack a few belongings, but I move slowly. I can't make decisions on what to bring. My husband sees me struggling and holds me. I bury my head in his chest and allow myself to fall limp in his arms. My tears flow.

Rachel comes with us. I'm very grateful for her assistance. We drive in silence to Indian Head, Maryland. My world has collapsed. I start to make up stories in my head. *Maybe he didn't die. Maybe it's all a mistake. Maybe he took off his dog tags to take a shower and someone else put them on and no one noticed that he had on the wrong ones. I just talked to him on Sunday. He can't be dead. My God wouldn't have let this happen!*

The day is quickly ending. It's now dark as we drive. I look out the window and for a brief second allow myself to consider the truth that my son is dead. *Where is he now, God? Can you show me?* I close my eyes and try to rest from my internal struggle. Suddenly, in a dreamlike state, I see Tony in his familiar, everyday clothes. He's standing next to Jesus with the biggest grin on his face. They're looking at me and have their arms around each other. My son says, "Mom, Mom, it's all true. Tell my family, my brothers and sisters it's all true. What you told me about God and His Word is all true!"

I make a strange sound as I contemplate what he's saying. I have been a Christian since I was twenty-one, and I've based my life on God, so I believe in Him. And yet at this moment, I'm filled with wonder. *Oh my! It's all true then. There is a God in heaven!*

The hair on my arms stands up as I contemplate what I've just heard. I gasp. My husband asks me what's wrong. I tell him what I saw. We drive the rest of the way in silence, but the vision plays over in my head, and I have a small sense of peace. Yet I am devastated.

I look at my husband; he is focused on the road. I haven't seen him cry. I wonder how he can act so completely normal.

I was twenty when I'd first heard about having a relationship with the Lord. My husband and I were living in Elmont, New York. His family lived in the Catskills in New York, and we lived about two hours away from his parents. Because we would visit the Catskills often, I had seen my mother-in-law, Millie, and her Christian friends dance, sing, and praise God. She would sing praises as she cleaned her kitchen. She seemed to know God, and that frightened me. Who can have a real relationship with God, the Creator of everything? I considered this and yet, deep inside, I too wanted to know God like that.

While we were stationed at Moody Air Force Base in Georgia, we went back to New York to visit my mother and father-in-law. At some point during the visit, Millie was leading a prayer meeting in her living room. I was curious. I stood just outside the living room and strained to hear what they were saying. Someone came out of the room and invited me into the meeting. Reluctantly, I walked in and sat on a couch. I was uncomfortable, a fish out of water. I planned on sneaking out when no one was looking, but the women were smiling at me. I couldn't leave. I decided to listen.

The meeting continued. One woman, Patty, stopped the prayers and said, "There is someone here who is very curious about the Lord but afraid. I see her sitting on a horse, and the Lord is standing in front of the horse holding the reins. She's leaning back and telling Jesus she's scared and doesn't want the horse to move. Jesus is gently encouraging her to come along, telling her that He'll hold the reins and take her along the path meant for her. Who is this person?"

I heard my heart beating. Without any conscious decision on my part, my hand flew up. I was astounded. The eight women gathered around me and started to pray. I was glad to see Nancy, my sister-in-law, among them. *They put their hands on me! What are they doing?*

I heard kind words spoken over me, and I started to relax. A strange heat started to come over me; I felt loved. I was five months pregnant at that time, and my new little one moved around in what I perceived to be leaps of joy. God had touched me and my soon-to-be-born son, Jason, with His Love.

I felt different. I wanted to confess Jesus as my Lord and be filled with His Spirit. The women instructed me through a prayer, and I was happy to comply. I was a new creation! I couldn't stop smiling!

It was the same smile I saw on my son's face in my dream. He was now forever complete in Christ, and he was so happy to be in God's love. I sense peace. I know Jesus is holding my son and will hold us while we walk this life out. We will have to experience our loss but with the knowledge the gospel is all true. I don't want the vision to end. I close my eyes. Tears run down my cheeks.

As we enter Indian Head Naval Base, my heart starts racing, pounding. *How can I see his wife and children?* I feel I will fall apart. Again I want to run. Hide. Retreat. I am dreading the encounter.

I see Angie outside with the children. I jump out of the car and fall into her arms. We hug. My husband walks up. He wants to help. He stammers, "Now we don't need to … we don't need to … this was … my son." He breaks down into tears. I let go of Angie and go to him. We hug. I hear the children—Mark, who's twelve; Tori, nine; Jared, six; Shawn, four; and Anna, just one—running around us. The younger children are so confused about what's happening. I want to help everyone, but I don't even know how to help myself.

We go inside their apartment. The sadness is overwhelming. I still want to believe that there's been some mistake, that this hasn't happened. I start to get calls from our adult children. They tell us how they heard the news. Mike happened to call when the military team was at the house. He was given a minute-by-minute account. Jason was home alone when his wife, Tricia, came home to tell him the news she had just received from Rachel. Jason felt he was so heavy that he could barely walk. James heard over the phone and broke down.

The children pack up their belongings and drive back to our house with my husband and Rachel. I stay with Angie. We talk. We decide to leave tomorrow after we pack up what the children will need. It's too much to take in. We're exhausted.

I ask her when she last heard from Tony. She says he called last night. She could hear noise from the bombings in the background. He told her he couldn't sleep. I tell her about my last conversation with him and how he told me he wanted to get out of the military and start a chicken farm. I had laughed about it; I thought he was joking, but maybe he was serious. He thought it would be a great adventure spending his days outdoors and enjoying a peaceful life.

We sit in silence at times, then we cry, then we go back to silence. At one point, Angie tells me we can have a service at my church. I tell her I would like that.

We are numb. We need to rest. I lie on Tony and Angie's bed. I see his clothing hanging in the closet. Again, I go into denial. I comfort myself with the dream I had earlier in the car. I think that when I wake up, it'll be all right—he'll be alive, and it will all have been a mistake.

I lie in the dark with my eyes wide open, not knowing what to do. Usually, I try to be strong and help our family deal with whatever's going on, but this is so far out of my understanding. I pray to God to help us all.

We wake up the next morning and pack clothes, toys, bottles, playpen, and different food for the children. I'm anxious to get home. I'm desperate to get some time with God.

We pull up to our home. I see children running across the lawn, three bikes in the driveway, and some wonderful chalk circles, squiggles, and pictures done by some obviously creative souls. Life seems so normal. *How can this be?* Life continues even though I feel time has stopped. *Doesn't everyone know?* I start to cry.

The house is full of noises; I need some quiet. My husband asks me how I'm doing. I barely answer him as I step over toys, dirty clothes, and books strewn all over the place. Kids are running in and out of the house. It's controlled chaos. I smile at our little grandchildren. My heart aches for them. The effects of their dad's death will be a lifelong journey for them.

I tell everyone I'm going to lie down. I get in my room and close the door. I feel exhausted but don't understand why. Drifting off to sleep, I think about my son.

I remember a time when we were living in Cheyenne, Wyoming. The morning temperature there was a frigid ten below. I bundled my oldest son in mittens, scarf, heavy coat, and boots. His schoolbooks were in his backpack. Looking like a citizen of Greenland, he trudged off to wait for the school bus. I watched him from our front window. He was standing at the bus stop, plowed snow all around him. The school bus was very late that day. I grabbed my coat, boots, and hat and went out to join him. After a few minutes, I saw the bus coming. Because of the huge snowdrifts, the driver couldn't see us. He passed our stop, and the children in the bus saw Tony and me. They pointed at Tony and laughed.

I was furious at the thought of my sweet little guy being laughed at. All moms want to protect their children. Even after our children become adults, that feeling of wanting to protect them never leaves.

I felt then that my daily prayers for God's protection were a way I could keep him safe. But I can't protect Tony ever again. I feel such a loss. He was an adult, and yet I can't stop wanting to protect him.

The next day is Julia's birthday. She's turning ten, and she's excited about what presents she will receive. The last thing I want to do is celebrate a birthday, but I know it's important to her.

My pastor, Ernest, and his wife, Mary, come by for a visit the next day. After dinner, we pile onto the back deck and sing "Happy Birthday." Over twenty family members are there. I'm standing next to Julia. I have my hand on her shoulder, but I suddenly feel the need to escape. I can't be there. My heart is too heavy. I pull back. Mary sees me struggling. She hugs me, and I sob as the party continues. Hugging Julia on her birthday brings me such peace; I need to feel something. Sometimes, even the smallest acts are so significant to us.

I realize no one is going to completely understand my pain just as I can't fully understand Angie's or my husband's pain. I know we'll have to deal with this individually. I determine at that moment to keep talking to God and to start a journal. Having no clue what to do, I choose to say a simple sentence over and over in my mind: *I'm going to be stronger when I get through this than when I started.* I feel compelled to say it even though it makes absolutely no sense. I don't want to be stronger when I get through this.

During the following week, all our adult children come home. Jason, Tricia, and their two children are the first to arrive. Jason, our second-born son, is also in the Air Force. He attends the Uniformed Services University of the Health Sciences in Bethesda, Maryland, and will graduate as a medical doctor after he finishes a residency in San Antonio. It's such a comfort to see them. Tricia is posting wonderful messages about Tony on her blog to keep everyone updated. We all hug and laugh as Jason tells many funny stories about Tony, like how he could eat a whole stick of butter in one sitting. He had such a great sense of humor. Even at this very desperate time, we're still thinking about all the funny things he did. We all go to bed. We all yearn to see him once again.

My fourth-born son, Michael, arrives from Oklahoma next and immediately gets to work with his dad doing things around the house. Michael is also in the Air Force; he received an engineering degree from the University of Portland and is working with military and civilian satellites and payloads.

Soon after, James and his fiancée, Tish, arrive from Germany. They are in the Air Force as well. James graduated from the University of Portland and entered the military soon after. While in Germany, he met an amazing woman in his same career. They do volunteer work with a youth group and accompany teens on mission trips.

My husband is the oldest of seven: Nancy, Jim, Ralph, Mike, Louis, and Doug. They all call to ask what they can do to help. They tell us they'll be here for the funeral, and we're very grateful for that.

Louis, my husband's brother, is the first of his brothers and sisters to come, and he helps us around the house. My husband's mother, Millie, calls to pray with my husband. She tells him about a vision she had of Tony, a vision of a loving and caring Jesus hugging him. I cry when I hear how she explains it. I want to hug him too. *Oh, Jesus, help me.*

When my family hears about Tony, they call and support me; I feel I have so little strength. I have four brothers—John, Jim, Paul, and Mark. They tell me they will be there for me. My dad explains that my mom won't be able to come for the funeral but he'll be there.

The house is alive with activity. At times during the day, I allow myself to hide in my bedroom. I pull out Tony's baby pictures and look at each one. I don't know what I should do other than talk to God and tell him how I'm feeling. We wait to hear when Tony's body will be returning from Iraq. The wait seems endless.

I keep saying to myself, *I'm am going to be stronger when I get through this than when I started* even though I still don't know what that means.

I now believe it was a way to bring some type of hope to a desperate situation. It was such a powerful statement of faith that sustained me countless times since then.

CHAPTER 1

Celebration of His Life

In Iraq, the soldiers Tony served with had a memorial service for him. It was a typical service soldiers hold to give tribute to their departed friends and fellow soldiers. We received a video from the military. Some family members couldn't watch it, but the few of us who did watched it in silence.

The first thing we saw in the video was his name in bold print set on a blue screen. We see a big, white tent with many service members from different branches of the military coming in and standing by something against one wall. We saw what they were looking at, and I cried. His boots were on a pedestal with his rifle standing upright between his boots. On the top of the rifle was his helmet. A picture of Tony was on a pedestal next to his memorial. I watched his comrades place medals and other memorabilia on an area near his boots. Some soldiers saluted, and some knelt. It was moving. I was amazed at their response to his death. A chaplain gave a passionate eulogy. We watched soldiers go up to say their farewells. We turned off the video in silence.

Tony's body was flown to Dover Air Force Base. As is the case with all fallen soldiers, his journey to the mortuary there began in the hold of a cargo plane that was met by military officials. A member of the military had been assigned to accompany his body to his resting place.

The coffin had a flag over it, and a team of about six carried the coffin off the plane to a white van that took his remains to the Air Force medical examiner for an official autopsy. When the autopsy was completed, mortuary services began its job.

They clean bodies and prepare them for the loved ones to say their last farewells. After the bodies are prepared, the mortuary staff prepares the soldiers with their dress uniforms and all their appropriate medals and rank placed on it. If the coffins are to be closed at the funerals, the uniforms are placed on top of the body.

Tony's coffin was sealed. We learned his uniform was on top of his body. On April 12, his body was delivered to Covenant Funeral Home, which contacted us. We had a viewing for my son on April 15. My husband, Angie, and I had gone the day before to talk about the details. I wanted to see Tony Jr. I kept asking my family about it. Everyone told me that it would be better for me to remember Tony as he was rather than as he looked in the coffin. Maybe it was my way of saying good-bye, or maybe it was a way to come to grips with the sorrowful situation, but I couldn't stop asking. The director was very kind. He asked if we wanted a family service. I was the one who wanted that. We decided to have one the next day.

My husband and I drove to the funeral home in silence the next day. I was numb. Only the adults came to the funeral home. My heart was beating so hard when we pulled into the parking lot. I could barely breathe. I got out of the car, but my feet were so heavy that I had trouble lifting them.

When we got into the lobby, the director told us to wait until they came for us. I sat and watched our family come in. Finally, the director brought us to the room. He opened the door. I saw the coffin at the far end of the room. I felt compelled to walk to the coffin. I put my hand on it. It was draped with the American flag. I was in a bad dream. Angie also touched the coffin. Pastor Ernest was with her. I put my head on top of the coffin and said, "Tony, you taught me to be a mom." I wept from deep inside. I was in the moment; I felt agony and despair.

My brother-in-law Mike put his hand on my shoulder as I cried. He escorted me to a chair. With tears streaming down my face, I looked around the room. Everyone was talking quietly among themselves. I looked at the flowers surrounding the casket. We had been blessed with some beautiful displays and caring messages from all over. I saw my three sons—Jason, Mike, and James—kneeling in front of the casket with their hands on the flag and praying.

Slowly, everyone started to leave. I asked the director how much time was set aside for the viewing. He said we had until 8:00 p.m., and it was only 5:30 p.m. My husband wanted to know if I was ready to go home since everyone had left. I couldn't leave my son. I pulled an overstuffed chair in front of his casket and sat. I wasn't going to leave one second earlier than 8:00 p.m. Tony was going to have visitors to the last minute. I knew it didn't make any sense, but I didn't care. My husband saw how determined I was to stay, so he walked out to call the family and tell them we were staying.

When I was alone in the room, I stood up and straightened the flag. I stood in front of the casket and sobbed. I had to see him one more time. It was all so final. I had to see him again. I put my hands on the lid and tried with all my might to open it. It was firmly sealed. It didn't budge. "Oh Lord, please let me see him again," I cried. I hated the finality of it all.

My husband came back. Soft music was playing in the background, and my husband and I held each other. It reminded me of when Tony Jr. was born. After all the busyness of the birth, they brought him to us. We enjoyed time as new parents, holding him and getting to know him. The moment at the funeral home was a little time cut out of eternity during which we spent time for the last time on this side of heaven with our firstborn. My husband and I sat with Tony until the last minute.

The funeral was planned for April 16. We went to our church, Grace Church in Fredericksburg, to talk to Pastor Ernest about the service. We needed to make many decisions—the format of the service, the music, even the type of bulletin to hand out. I was physically and emotionally exhausted.

Jason and Tricia helped prepare a video for the service; they had brought with them all the pictures and music they needed for that. It was nice not to have that work on my shoulders. I didn't have the energy.

When I got home, I went straight to my bedroom. More and more of our family started to arrive, and it was getting very busy. I needed to retreat and allow myself some time to process the whole event. The back deck was filled with family and friends. I looked through more of his pictures and prayed for our family and for strength.

My husband would come in the bedroom, sit with me, cry, and go back out to spend time with the family. At one point, I walked out the French doors that led to the deck with some of Tony's pictures in hand. I threw the pictures out the door and said, "This just hurts!" I saw the photos scattered on the floor. I saw Tony's cute baby face looking at me in one photo, and I snatched them all up and ran back to the bedroom. I started saying, "I will be stronger when I get through this than when I started."

So many people came to pray for, feed, and support us—especially people from our church. I felt the presence of God carrying us all through those days. It was as if we were on life support in an ICU. Many friends called to give us encouraging messages. One school in Maryland sent us over a hundred messages on decorated three-by-five cards students had written.

My father came, but he couldn't bring my mom. She was in the last stages of Alzheimer's, and it was better for her to stay in the assisted care facility, but I really wanted her there with me. My husband's five brothers and their wives and families all came, as did his only sister, Nancy, and her husband. We were surrounded with the love of our family, and that was so important to us all.

One morning, I woke up early. The sun was rising. I took a deep breath and walked outside. It was so quiet and peaceful; it was probably the first time since my son had died that I felt a little more like myself. I laid a blanket on the grass and sat with my Bible. I needed quiet time. I prayed my typical prayers for my children, starting with the oldest. I must have prayed that way over a million times, but I began with Tony's name and stopped. I groaned as I realized I never had to pray for him again. But how could I pray for my children without mentioning him? I buried my face in the blanket and cried. All day long, I had memories of words spoken and pictures of Tony I looked at. I was in a box filled with pain.

I suddenly stopped crying and looked to the sky. I didn't understand how I was going to make it through this, but I had to believe I would be stronger when I got through this than when I started. I was on a trip with no GPS. I had to believe God loved me and would hold me close. I grabbed a pencil and wrote this poem on a stray piece of paper that happened to be in my Bible.

Love Is Your Heart

You are my Father
Strength and courage
Are Your clothing for me
And love is Your heart
Wrap me up in your arms
As I spend time with you
I gain Your strength
I feel Your heartbeat
For myself and others
And love is your heart
My Daddy is calling
Me by name
He wants me to come to Him

5

He tells me I am precious
And to be brave
And love is His heart
He says "No matter what
Storm or situation
I will be there with you
Each day I will carry you in my arms
And love is My heart"

—Sharon Capra

On April 26, we held the service for Tony's funeral. It was a pretty day. The local American Legion had offered to place fifty small flags across the front of the lawn so those driving by could see the flags standing at attention. The flags were waving peacefully in the gentle April breeze, yet inside, everyone was busy trying to get ready.

Sarah, Joe, Jacob, Danielle, Joanna, Julia, Emily, my husband, and I piled into our extended van. As we drove to the church, we were silent, not knowing what to say, think, or feel.

As we approached the church, the anticipation mounted. The silence in the car hung heavily. We turned into the parking lot, and the church came into view. Twenty members of the Patriot Guard were standing shoulder to shoulder in front of the church. Each had an American flag and was standing at full attention, watching and waiting to honor the fallen soldier and his family.

The Patriot Guard is an organization of volunteers who form honor guards for the funerals of military members, firefighters, and police officers at the invitation of the families of the deceased. They took my breath away. Their act of service at my son's funeral was so moving. Their motorcycles parked in the lot were decorated with small flags.

Tony parked the car in front of the church, and we all headed in. We were greeted by an attendant who told us the family should gather in the church café. The family would enter the sanctuary at the beginning of the service.

I saw my friends gathering in small circle and speaking quietly while others were signing the guest book. I saw many people seated in the sanctuary and the flag-draped coffin in front. My heart hurt to see the coffin. It was surreal.

Family members started to arrive and gather in the café. We were numb. My cousins sat with me. I was surrounded by family. A member of the Veterans of Foreign Wars came into the café and handed each of us a flag memorial pin. Pastor Ernest gave us instructions on how we were going to enter the service.

After twenty minutes, we were escorted into the sanctuary. The music began. Pastor Ernest led the procession with Angie and the five grandchildren following him. Next came Tony and I followed by our children. The church was filled. Everyone stood as we entered. I saw my friends, neighbors, and family watch us walk to the front. The first five rows were reserved for us. I saw the coffin draped with the flag, and I felt a burning sensation in my heart. I didn't know what to do. I saw big floral arrangements decorating the front. We heard piano music. I saw two poster-size pictures of Tony. I sighed and stifled a sad, mournful sound.

I saw my husband next to Angie and our five grandchildren. Behind me were my sons and daughters. EOD soldiers were to our left. We stood as the worship team started to play. We had planned the songs before the service. The music lifted my soul in prayer. I raised my hands in honor to God while looking at my son's coffin. *This is how it feels to acknowledge God when it looks like there's no hope.* The pastor walked up to the front, introduced himself, and gave the sermon.

Pastor Ernest announced that my friend Lydia was going to sing Psalm 23 in Hebrew and in English. It moved everyone in the whole church; it connected me to my son in a way I can't explain. People were given a time to say their remembrances. At the end of the service, Jason, James, Michael, Joe, and Jacob brought their brother's coffin down the aisle. We followed the procession and watched the boys load the casket into the back of the hearse. *Can this possibly get any harder?*

We got into the limo with Mark, Tori, Jared, Shawn and Anna. The twenty Patriot Guard men and women were on their motorcycles ready to go. The hearse was next, followed by our limousine. We slowly left the parking lot and turned onto the main road. Police had stopped all traffic; we had clearance through each intersection.

It was quiet in the limo. We were all numb and dreaded what was to come. I looked at our grandchildren and thought about how their lives had forever been changed. We got on I-95, one of the main highways on the East Coast. I took a deep breath. I was on a trip I didn't want to be on, and I couldn't get off. It reminded me of being strapped into a roller-coaster. You desperately want to get off, but it keeps going. There's no way to stop it.

All three lanes on I-95 North were empty though it was typically congested. I saw the Patriot Guard's motorcycles, flags waving in the wind, leading the way. Our limo followed, and the funeral procession drove behind us in single file. Our driver pulled into the far left lane. I saw normal traffic on I-95 South. *What's going on here?* I'd lived in the area for over seven years but had never seen I-95 North plain empty.

As we passed the first entry ramp, I saw a police car that had stopped traffic from getting on. The officer stood at attention and saluted as we passed. I realized the only traffic on I-95 North was our funeral procession. *We're sixty miles from Arlington National Cemetery. How long will this police escort go on?* I marveled at what God had done for us. I thought of the verse in Ephesians that says He gives us more than we can think or imagine. It was unbelievable; each mile was the same. The roadway was clear except for our funeral procession, which was more than a mile long. I marveled that a police officer was saluting at each entry ramp. I heard a traffic helicopter reporting the situation on I-95.

When we neared Springfield, a police motorcycle motorcade entered I-95; the riders positioned themselves in front of the Patriot Guard. We drove past Bypass 495, and again, there was no traffic allowed on I-95. Though my heart was grieving, I was astounded.

When we arrived at Arlington, I held my breath. It was such a notable place. My parents had taken me there when I was thirteen; I hadn't been back since then, but I remembered the solemn atmosphere of the cemetery, which had been established on May 13, 1864.

Its 624 acres are divided into seventy sections. An estimated 400,000 active duty personnel, veterans, and family members are interred in Arlington. Around thirty funerals take place every week. Many visitors come to see the Tomb of the Unknown Soldier and the grave sites of John F. Kennedy, Robert Kennedy, and so many more. One noteworthy woman laid to rest there was Juliet Hopkins, called the Florence Nightingale of the South for her brave and generous acts during the Civil War. Arctic explorer Admiral Perry is also interred there. More than four million people visit Arlington each year, a place that evokes awe, respect, and dignity.

Our procession entered Memorial Gate, which is lined with many memorials and a visitors' center that displays the history and memorable moments of the cemetery. The main road leads to the Women in Military Service for America memorial. Rising behind the memorial on a hill is Arlington House. The police motorcade pulled to the side and saluted as we drove toward the inside of the cemetery. In the limousine, we sat in complete silence, but I was crying on the inside. We pulled up in front of the family reception center and walked into the building. I searched for my husband, who hadn't arrived. I ran to the bathroom and didn't want to come out. I needed time to pray and ask God to help me with the day.

When I came out, I saw so many people gathered in the room. My husband walked up and wrapped his arm around me. I was relieved to be near him, but everyone was talking to us, and I was uncomfortable. I didn't know what to think or how to react to people. I wanted to hide, but there was no escape. Although I was devastated, I felt the need to talk with those around me. My husband introduced me to some of his coworkers. Everyone was very friendly and nice, but I couldn't converse for long.

The director gave us directions; he said that only the family limousine would be allowed to park by the grave site. Everyone else was to walk from the administration building to the grave site.

Angie looked at me. I walked to her. We gathered her precious children and entered the limousine while the rest of the guests began walking down the road to the grave site. It was a beautiful April day. Virginia was typically cool that time of year, but that day was atypical. The sun was so intense; it felt like June. The limo waited for Angie's mom and sister. I saw everyone walking down the path, talking and acting normally. *Do any of them understand I want all life to stop because my son died?*

The hearse was ahead of us as we drove to the grave. Our car was barely moving. Maybe I was just barely breathing and life had indeed slowed down. We turned down York Street—named after Sergeant York, the most decorated World War I soldier. I saw grave after grave lined up in perfect formation. It reminded me of soldiers standing at attention. A large crowd had gathered.

I hesitantly climbed out and stood behind Angie. I saw soldiers in full-dress uniforms pulling the coffin out of the hearse. My tears flowed. Along the opposite side of the street was a huge crowd of friends, coworkers, and family watching and supporting us on this painful journey. The flag-draped coffin was brought to the grave site and placed on a metal frame. Pastor Ernest followed the procession and motioned for Angie to follow him. She looked at me to follow behind her. I walked slowly; I was living and breathing in each second. I couldn't think of anything but the moment I was in. Running away was not an option. The large crowd moved in behind us. I learned later that over a thousand people had attended.

The coffin was beautifully decorated with the American flag draped over it. Next to the grave were four rows of chairs on outdoor carpeting. Angie, two of her children, Tony, and I sat in the first row. Pastor Ernest stood next to the coffin, and our immediate family filled in the three rows of chairs. It was so bright that I had to keep my sunglasses on. I was glad because my eyes were so red from all the crying; I could hide behind them. I knew it was only an illusion; no one can hide from the stark reality of death.

The service started. After the pastor read some Scriptures and prayed, bagpipes played "Amazing Grace." The music floated on the breeze. The song was a temporary balm for my soul, a brief escape from what was going on around me. I wanted it never to end. It was the worst moment of my life, but I wasn't ready to move. It was the last time on earth I'd be next to my son's body. I thought of Mary who went to the cross where her Son was dying. It was so horrible for her to look, but she had to stay. That was her baby, the one she held so close and loved. She had to stay because it involved her personally. I understood that; that part of Scripture made sense to me for the first time. The music faded away. Silence fell upon us all.

Then *boom, boom, boom*—the three-volley salute. I jumped as each round went off. Seven members of the military fired a total of twenty-one times. I heard that during certain heated American battles in our past, opposing armies had to make sure all the dead had been properly taken off the field after hours of battle. The three-volley salute would temporarily end the fighting.

I looked at my son's casket and thought about how the military had ensured that his burial had been a proper and dignified farewell. I saw so many gravestones shining in the bright sun and realized everyone who had been laid to rest there had had a service and that those attending had heard the same gun salute. How somber. My mind was reeling; my tears kept coming. There was no way to stop crying, and I had no desire to.

The honor guard strode to the casket, four men on each side. They pulled the flag up and over the coffin and folded it in silence. It was a major ritual in military funerals. According to the American Legion, there is meaning for each fold. The first is the symbol of life, the second is a symbol of our belief in eternal life, and the third is for the remembrance of the fallen soldier and for the defense of our country to attain peace throughout the world.

The fourth fold represents our weaker nature as American citizens trusting in God, to whom we turn in times of peace as well as war for His guidance. The fifth is a tribute to our country. The sixth is for where our hearts lie; we pledge allegiance to the flag of the United States of America and to the republic for which it stands, one nation under God, indivisible, with liberty and justice for all.

The seventh fold is a tribute to our armed forces, which protect our country and our flag. The eighth fold is a tribute to the mothers of the United States. The ninth is a tribute to women, for it is through their faith, love, loyalty, and devotion that our country is so great.

The tenth is a tribute to the fathers of the United States who have given their sons and daughters for the defense of our nation. The eleventh fold is for the laws of our nation, the twelfth is to honor God, and the thirteenth is when the flag is completely folded in the shape of a triangle. The blue part of the flag with the stars is visible. This reminds us of our country's motto, "In God We Trust."

The folded flag is tucked in and presented to the family. The first flag was presented to Angie, and a second flag was presented to me. Later, a third flag was presented to Tony and Angie's firstborn son, Mark. A fourth was presented to Jason, Tony's closest brother.

The playing of "Taps" is perhaps the most moving event of a military funeral service. Solemn and touching, the song affects all. The Virginia American Legion erected a memorial for the song on July 4, 1969.

I watched all our children walk up to the casket one by one to say a prayer or think quietly. My heart was so heavy. I thought about how much I wanted my mom to be there; I longed for her comfort and hugs. I was numb, hurting, and vulnerable.

I feel a hand on my shoulder, and I turn around. It's BJ! I'd met BJ many years ago. She was a dear friend to my husband's mother, and she was a precious friend to me. I reached out to her and sobbed as she wrapped her loving arms around me. I felt safe, and I stayed in her arms for a while. I said, "Oh BJ! I can't believe you're here. I'd just thought about how much I needed a mother's hug, and here you are."

She smiled and gathered me back into her arms. I cried on her shoulder. It was a moment of peace at a very disturbing time. I thanked God under my breath. I was so grateful that God had allowed her to come all the way from New York to be there at just the right moment to hug me. BJ couldn't stay long, but her visit was a gift from God.

I looked at the last family member laying roses on Tony's coffin. Friends, coworkers, and other family took turns going up to the coffin. Some stopped and said a short prayer. When the military coworkers went up, they took off a pin or ripped off their armbands and laid them on the coffin. After laying down their honorary symbols, they stepped back and saluted my son. I cried each time. My son had done amazing things in his life to cause so many people to honor him.

I refused to leave that spot until everyone who wanted to come up had had the opportunity to do so. One of my daughters told me it was time to leave. I refused. I wasn't ready to let go of that moment. I felt that if I stayed there, I could somehow stop all this from continuing. I heard people talking quietly around me, but I stood there firmly rooted in the ground.

I was to be the last person in our family to walk to the coffin and say good-bye, but I just couldn't do it. I wasn't ready. If I didn't say good-bye, time would stand still. I wanted it to. I laid my hand on his coffin gently and carefully. I looked at all the flowers, pins, ribbons, and military patches people had left on Tony's coffin. He would have loved to have seen all the people here. He was such a people person. I told my son that I didn't want this. My husband gently escorted me to the car, but I didn't want to leave my son. I wanted to make sure they buried him right.

As the car pulled away, I saw the cemetery staff getting ready to place the coffin in the ground. I couldn't stop looking until his grave site was out of view. I sighed as we began the drive home. I had never experienced such sadness.

I was reminded of the biblical Rizpah, a concubine of Saul. David had avenged the Gibeonites by hanging seven of Saul's descendants. Two of them were sons of Rizpah. They were hung and left to be a reminder that David had avenged the Gibeonites.

> Now Rizpah the daughter of Aiah took sackcloth and spread it for herself on the rock, from the beginning of the harvest until the late rains poured on them from heaven. And she did not allow the birds of the air to rest on them by day nor the beasts of the field by night. (2 Samuel 21:10)

She protected them day and night. When King David heard about this, he buried the bodies of Saul and his sons. He felt compassion for her. She finally went home to grieve.

We mothers have taken care of our children since we carried them in our wombs. Even after they move out, we continue to be concerned for their safety, happiness, and well-being. It's unnatural to be released from that role earlier than expected. Maybe this is why children are supposed to outlive their parents. When a child dies, no matter what the age, it's as though a part of us has died and been buried along with the child we lay to rest.

As the limo pulled out of the cemetery, I struggled with the issue of leaving. *I shouldn't leave until I'm sure that they've buried him properly.* When a mother drops off her toddler at a nursery and the child cries out for her, her heart tells her to run back, pick up her child, and leave. But there was no way I could go back and get Tony. Even if I screamed for the limo driver to take me back to his grave, I couldn't bring him home. There wasn't a thing I could do but go home.

The drive home was so different. The children were getting tired. They started drinking the soda in the back of the limo. Once we got onto I-95 South, I saw that the northbound traffic was very congested due to the road closure for our procession earlier. No police officers saluted us at every ramp. Reality started to sink in. It was all over. I felt that in my soul. I sat in silence as the children played. Was I the one who had died? It seemed that the world had stopped for an afternoon and then, as soon as it could, it came back in a fury.

The limo driver dropped us off. Many people had blessed us with a variety of delicious treats that were in the dining room. The smells were enticing, but I didn't feel like eating. I retreated to my bedroom and asked God for help getting through the afternoon. I took off my dress and threw it in the trash. I never wanted to wear it again. I realized I had to socialize; the sounds of laughter and people talking seemed cheerful. I told myself to go out there and smile and be nice. Our family and friends were there to help us get through this, but I realized only God could do that. "God, please help me," I whispered under my breath as I walk out of my bedroom.

People continued to pour into our house. I saw many cars in the driveway. My husband was busy helping the servers with all the wonderful food. I could see that it made him feel better to help with the food. He gave me a hug. Pastor Ernest came in; we made small talk, and I thanked him for all his help. We talked about the wonderful escort we'd had to Arlington and how I-95 had been cleared for us. He'd been in the front of the procession and had seen police chase stray cars off the interstate. I thought of Ephesians: 3:20 "Now to Him who is able to do exceedingly abundantly above all that we ask or think according to the power that works in us." It was a miraculous sight I knew I'd remember forever'. What a tribute to all servicemen and women who have given their lives for our country.

I made small talk and retreated frequently to my bedroom, but I was comforted by all the loving, caring people who had come to show their care for us. I thanked God for each one. My father and four brothers, Paul, Mark, Jim, and John, came to the house as well; it was such a blessing to have them there. Our whole extended family helped us out tremendously.

The reception ended in the early evening. We were all exhausted. After the guests left, our house seemed hollow, empty. I tried to fall asleep in the recliner with a blanket, but so many thoughts raced through my mind. *What's supposed to happen now? Is it all over? Is it okay to still be feeling such loss?* Tears cascaded over my face as I drifted into a fitful sleep.

When I woke the next morning, I felt as though I hadn't slept at all. The activity in the house had started already. I knew that the weekend was over and all our family and friends would leave. It was so sad to see them go. I felt lonely. I thought about all that had happened the past few days. It was as if my body had floated through all the events while my heart had refused to accept the reality of it all.

On May 20, 2008, I received a phone call from Angie. She told me they had found more remains of our son after his body was returned to us. DNA tests verified it was Tony. The mortuary services needed to know what Angie wanted to do with the remains. She called my husband. After they talked, they decided to place the newfound remains in the same grave site at Arlington. I refused to think about it.

Arlington National Cemetery arranged a date for a second funeral service on July 15. My husband went to work that day and planned to meet Angie and me at Arlington around noon. I called Pastor Ernest; he said he would accompany Angie and me. We gathered at the administration building in Arlington and waited for the clerk to tell us when to go to the grave site. I was quiet. It was truly awful. We were told to go to Section 60, where the hearse would be shortly. I told my pastor I was having a very hard time with this. *Why would God make me go through this a second time?*

When we arrived, the ground was dug up around Tony's site, and four chairs rested on that familiar green carpet. The hearse pulled up. Three soldiers climbed out. One, in full, official dress, opened the back door, took out a small coffin, and carried it with honor and respect. My heart melted. A deep groan came out of my mouth. I felt unable to move. I watched Pastor Ernest, Angie, and my husband walk behind the soldier carrying the coffin. Angie grabbed my hand. I wept. We sat in the chairs. The small coffin was placed on a stand covered by green fabric. The name "Capra" was on a piece of masking tape on the coffin.

How different it was from the first funeral; seven people, no bagpipes, no gun salute, no crowds of support. Pastor Ernest said a prayer. I contemplated how beyond terrible it was. My wound that had just started to heal was reopened, and it was cut even deeper. *Why is God making me go through this a second time? Couldn't He have made sure all my son had been brought home at the same time?* I was crushed beneath the weight of the moment.

Then I thought of the Scripture that says when we're weak, He is strong. I asked my husband to pray for us because we were at our weakest just then. He prayed, and I prayed, "Thank you, Lord, for the son you gave Tony and me. Give us your strength and guidance to go on." I addressed our son. "I will always treasure you in my heart."

We heard a three-volley salute and "Taps" playing for another family. We got out of our chairs. Tony and Angie looked at the headstone. I saw my husband wipe off pieces of grass that had clung to it. I walked to the small coffin. *This is it. This is absolutely the last time I'll be so near to any remains of my son.* I place my hands on it and thank God for the gift of my son. I hear everyone else talking softly. I say boldly, "And yet again will I praise God the maker of heaven and earth." After a few minutes of talking and crying, we get back into our cars.

On the way home, I thought about how our son had had the biggest and then the smallest funeral I'd ever witnessed. Tears streamed down my face; I couldn't stop them if I had wanted to. My daughters took me out for lunch. I cried the whole time. I made no sounds of grief; I was very familiar with those sounds. My tears flowed. The food was not very tasty, and I felt defeated, but I sensed a tiny thread of hope somewhere in the midst of everything, a hope that could come only from God.

When I got home, I retreated to my bedroom and sobbed. My husband and I held each other. It was like pulling a scab off a wound and watching pus and blood flow out. I knew God was not mean. He had known this would happen. I knew God moved in our lives to make us whole and to give us back our dignity. I saw no answer just then, but I hung on to what I knew about God.

The following year, we were invited to Eglin Air Force Base in Florida. Every year, the EOD Memorial staff there invites the families of the fallen EOD from all military branches to a solemn ceremony during which the names of the fallen are placed on the wall of the memorial. It was a very touching and profoundly respectful ceremony.

Tony was honored by the EOD technicians at Eglin AFB. They dedicated the road that wrapped around their building to him. They had a wonderful ceremony; we were so moved by their kindness. Also at Indian Head, Maryland, another group of EOD technicians had a wing in an EOD building named in his honor.

I'm not the same person I was before that fateful day, April 9, 2008. I had to learn to walk, talk, and live again. However, I wasn't alone. Jesus was there every second of every day and tenderly leading me. Praise God!

CHAPTER 2

My Grief for a Year

This chapter is a diary I kept for the first year following Tony's death. I didn't alter it to make it sound better. It's messy with emotion. Some days, I would sense God's presence in the morning, but by the end of the day, I felt so alone. I pray that you observe the route I took during that first year as I hung on with all my might to my heavenly Daddy.

It was a tough year for me, but I am stronger now; I can say with assurance that God can help those who are hurting after the death of a loved one. What we experience in our walk of faith gives us strength to proclaim His truth; I can boldly proclaim that He can help you too.

Some events in life are plain hard, but we're not alone on our journey. I wish I could give you a hug, but I'm certain God is placing people around you right now to give you that hug, kiss, or ear. Look around and see His intimate provision for you.

April 23

Went to my home group at a church elder's home. I walked in and felt so weak. Everyone greeted me, but I had no energy. We started to sing, and for a few moments, my heart wanted to sing, but I cried. When we sat for the teaching, I was a child who was comforted by the sounds of the voices but who didn't recognize the meaning of the words.

April 27

Went to Grace Church, my home church, for the first time since the funeral. I sat quietly and looked over to where my son's coffin had been. A pain hit my mind as I remembered. The music started, and everyone began to sing. I stood up and joined. Suddenly, my daughter Sarah pushed past me and ran up to the front of the church and started to dance. I was mesmerized as I watched the beautiful motions of a heart rejoicing before God. How I wished I too could run up there and join her. It was marvelous to watch a person respond with reckless abandonment to show love toward God. She was truly an amazing sight.

I closed my eyes and let my heart drift on the note of the songs. I had a vision of Tony and me sitting on God's lap. We were facing a huge congregation. I saw many people of all different races gathered in unity. They were all praising God, and I was enthralled with what I saw. Tony leaned to me and whispered, "Mom, Mom, I now know some of the plans that God has for you, and they're awesome. You'll have to get up and walk so you can accomplish what He has for you." He looked so peaceful—not a care in the world. "Why are you whispering?" I asked. He said, "I don't know." We looked up at God, who was smiling at us.

God is a caring Father who smiles in love at his children and holds them in their darkest times.

April 28

Very sad today. I want my son home.

April 29

I woke up and thought of one of my friends, Lauren. She had come to our house and helped us out. I called her, and she invited me over. I drove to her house with an expectation that God would help me somehow. There was no reason to have hope, but I did.

When she saw me at the door, she gave me a big hug and welcomed me into her home. I sat at the kitchen bar, and Lauren gave me a cup of tea. We walked down to her basement prayer room, and we prayed together. Listening to her advice, I took some deep breaths. It was an oasis in the desert, and I was comforted.

May 1

Lauren sent me an email with an awesome word from the Lord. I printed a copy of it and put it in my Bible.

May 2

Got out of bed and didn't know what to do with myself. I sat with my Bible in my lap and declared, "You won, God! I declare this to all the demonic forces and the host in heaven—God has won. I am not defeated. I am not defeated because of what God has done. I am whole, restored, and complete."

My friend from New York, Nancy Wren, called me; she was coming to visit me.

May 3

Went to Arlington Cemetery. I didn't even have the car in park before I began to weep. I never thought I would visit the grave site of a Christian. After all, only the body was there; the person's spirit was alive with the Lord. But there I was. I was actually comforted to be there. I found that strange. How could anyone find comfort in a cemetery?

I met Amie, a woman who was visiting her brother's grave. She shared with me that there was a nonprofit called TAPS (Tragedy Assistance Program for Survivors) that helps those who have lost loved ones in war. She pointed out to me that there were small stones on some of the grave markers. They were signs of remembrance.

It reminded me of the Israelites who had used stone markers to remember what God had done.

I placed a stone where my son's name marker was and thought about how God had taken my son from this life to His life in heaven. I was grateful, but my heart was heavy. It saddened me to look down at the place where they had buried my son. I refused to walk on the ground that had been dug so recently. I didn't want to walk on his body.

May 4

My friend, Nancy Wren, arrived from New York, and we went to downtown Fredericksburg. A trolley tour bus takes visitors around to all the historic Civil War sites. The driver was very knowledgeable, and it was a nice day. He showed us many of the sites where soldiers had died. I thought about all the young people who had died for our country. My son was among their ranks. It all took on a different meaning.

May 5

Cried as I watched the DVD of the funeral. I relived every emotion I had felt during the service.

May 6

Woke up and started to pray. I felt I needed to find some peace in my morning. *What do I expect out of my life?* The world may tell us that we can't make it, that we're just not strong enough, but God has a plan for us. I looked through the Bible to find what God says so I say what He says about me.

May 7

It was the day Tony was due back from Iraq. I thought about him all day and wished I could see him. I found comfort in knowing that one day I would see him again. I thought of how we had buried him. It was like a seed being planted. His life had been planted in good ground, and it would produce good fruit in our lives and the lives of those who knew him.

The song that gave me encouragement was "I Have a Maker" by Tommy Walker. I put my two grandsons, Jared and Shawn, to bed that night and sang them that song. I wanted them to know that even though their lives had been forever changed, they still had a heavenly Father who would always be there for them. He would never leave them no matter where they went in life.

May 8

God has won. Not the grave. I was not defeated. He was asking me not to let grief defeat me. God asks us to do only what is good for us to make us whole and give us back our dignity.

May 9

Having a tough day today. Tony Jr. would have been back from Iraq by now. I was angry, but I was determined to praise Him despite how sad I felt. I wanted to be alone. I just wanted to scream at everyone to get away from me. The house was a big mess, and no one seemed to understand how much I needed help.

May 11

Went to church today and went up front after the service to receive prayer. I purposed to receive His grace. Soon after I got home, I had to repent for acting as if I were the only person hurting over Tony's death. For some reason, I wanted everyone to know I was hurting more than anyone else. As I watched my daughter-in-law and grandchildren, I realized how selfish I have been. I realized my son had a different relationship with each of us, and each of us was dealing with our loss in different ways. Thank you for forgiving me, Lord.

May 12

I had a dental appointment today. The dental hygienist was getting ready to clean my teeth and was making small talk. She asked me questions about my children, and she asked how old my oldest was. Without warning, I burst into sobs and curled up in a fetal position in the dental chair. The hygienist ran out of the room and got the dentist. I calmed myself down. I heard the dentist explain why I had reacted the way I had. It came on so quick, and I was embarrassed, but I knew I couldn't help it. I was still in the process. Thank you, God, for helping me through all this!

Driving home, I thought about the beauty of creation. How many flowers had God made since the beginning of time? How many blades of grass? Countless numbers—and yet He never appears to get tired of what He has made. Even though one blade of grass appears identical to another, there are amazing differences between each blade. More important than grass blades, God has made us, and He never gets tired of us. What an amazing Creator! How many women, men, and children have lived on this planet? He doesn't get tired of making us, and each one of us is so amazing.

May 13

After a busy morning of cleaning and homeschooling, I took a nap. I said a prayer of thanks to God for my life. While sleeping, I had a dream. My son, Tony, was standing with his hand on my shoulder. I was on my knees with head down and eyes closed. I heard, "When believers are living in the Spirit, when they're praising God, when they're setting their minds on things above, the great cloud of witnesses can see them because He is the God of the living—the God of Abraham, Isaac, and Jacob." What a fantastic thought! We are all connected because of the Spirit of God. The Holy Spirit flows through all His children; those who have gone before us and those who are on earth.

May 14

Lauren invited me to her church for their Wednesday night service. I drove to the service in my son's car, which we had bought from Angie. I looked on the passenger side floor and saw a gum wrapper with a note Tony had written. Next to the brake, I saw his security badge. I looked at his picture and put it up to my cheek. Am I crazy? No, I'm not. I just miss him so much.

I entered the church, and Lauren walked up to me and gave me a hug. I sat next to her, and the service began. At the end of the teaching, the pastor asked if anyone wanted prayer. I went up, and a group of people surrounded me. The pastor laid his hand on my head. I immediately felt a blanket of love encircling me. I didn't want that moment to end. I felt such peace.

As I drove home, I thought about the evening. I still felt so peaceful. I slept well for the first time since April 9.

May 17

Brenda and Melissa came over to help me clean my house. What a great way to help those who are grieving! They were such a blessing to me, but I talked way too much about Tony. It made me feel so depressed when they left.

I was so tired. I have to remember that when I feel overwhelmed, it's all right to be quiet. I think I talked too much. Jesus, Jesus, Jesus, Your name is a strong tower, and I need Your strength. I love You, Jesus.

May 18

Went to church. It was the first time I was able to sing and join in with the praise and worship songs. It was so refreshing to my soul. Went to the cemetery after church. I cried. I miss him so much.

May 20

Went over to Angie's apartment. The Air Force delivered fifteen boxes of Tony's belongings from Iraq. We opened one box after the other. I found the Bible I had given him. I read what I had written in the front page. I cried as I read my prayer for his safety. I thumbed through the Bible and sobbed. I needed someone to hold me. I hugged Angie.

May 21

I flew down to Florida to help my dad. He was going to France to participate in the American Legion events during the D-Day commemorations. He used to take my mom with him, but her Alzheimer's had progressed to the point that she needed to stay home.

My mom looked the same, but her mind was gone. She still remembered who I was, but many of the experiences we had shared were memories of me alone. We could no longer carry on lengthy conversations over the phone. It was basically me just letting her talk.

In the airplane, I felt so unready to leave the comfort of my home and family. When I felt sad, I could retreat into my home. Now I had to rest in God's comfort. I still felt unsteady, but I buckled my seat belt for takeoff.

My dad picked me up at the airport. We made small talk. We stayed off the topic of Tony. I ask him about his upcoming trip. My mom was at home with my brother. When I saw her, she hugged me, but she disconnected a second later. I felt sad. *God help me. I don't think I'm ready for this. I still feel so weak. How can I take care of someone when I can't take care of myself?*

My dad left that night for France. My brother took him to the airport.

May 22

When people are searching for comfort, they tend to look for someone to fill the emptiness. I was looking to my mom to make me feel better. I searched her face to give me some look of understanding or some kind of tenderness. I tried desperately to tell her about my pain. I wanted her to know what had happened to my son.

The American Legion in Boca Raton had heard about Tony and wanted to help his family. They were going to have a fundraiser with food, games, and activities and give all the proceeds to Tony's family.

I visited the legion. They greeted, hugged, and loved me as I entered their building. I was touched by these men and women who wanted to help a grieving military spouse and children. It was amazing for me to hear all the plans they had for the event.

May 23

I woke up praying for God's help to get through the day. I dressed my mom, put a little lipstick on her, and put some breakfast on the table for her. She needed constant care. I sat across from her and looked at her. Her face was such a comfort to me, but where had my mom gone?

After breakfast, I drove her to the adult day care. I went back to her house. I was trying to find time alone with the Lord, but I struggled with my emotions. My brother and his wife were coming for a visit that weekend.

May 24

Started the day with prayer. Gave Mom a shower. She told me how wonderful it was to get her hair washed. I drive her to the Christian bookstore for a little while. Later, I put my mom down for a nap and I fell asleep on the couch.

May 25

Mark and Meg were at the house, so I decided to take the girls to the movies while they watched Mom. We went to see *Prince Caspian*. As I watched the battle scene in the movie, it reminded me of how important it was to put on our spiritual armor (Ephesians 5) to fight the good fight of faith. God won, not the Devil!

May 26

The Boca Raton American Legion had a memorial service at the military cemetery for Tony. We had to meet at 10:00 a.m. at the legion. My two brothers, Sandy, Meg, my mother, and I got there around 9:30 a.m. About twenty-five members of the legion arrived with their motorcycles and started attaching flags to the back of the seats.

Soon, a shiny limousine pulled up. We were told to get in. Two police cars came; the officers told us they would stop traffic between the legion and the cemetery. The legion members started up their motorcycles, their flags waving in the breeze. Police cars pulled in front of them to stop the traffic. It reminded me of the funeral procession but on a smaller scale.

When we arrived at the cemetery, we saw a tent over a platform filled with chairs. A small band was playing patriotic songs. We were escorted to the front row of chairs.

The service was very honorable and respectful. A World War II vet walked to the microphone and started the service. We stood during the national anthem, and I wept as I listened to the words.

At the end, people came over to my family and me to shake our hands and give their condolences. It was very nice. We were given a ride home with the escort, and they invited us to the legion for a nice lunch. I was so amazed at the kindness shown to my family by these veterans.

A big catastrophe can be a setup for a miraculous victory from God. I have a choice; I can look to God for my comfort or look to myself and others.

May 30

I needed to deal with my fear about someone else in my family dying. I had to resist fear and all the lies I'd listened to. I felt free from such thoughts. I declared my freedom. I spent six hours in prayer while my mom was at the adult day care. While I prayed, I walked down to the beach and watched waves crashing onto the shore. I expressed to God how I was feeling and asked Him how was I going to live without my son on earth. The ocean breeze and waves seemed so powerful, yet they were contained within limits. I remembered in the Bible where it said God decides how far the water is to go onto the shore. If God is that powerful, He can free me from my fear. I have to trust Him or I'll be too afraid to live.

May 31

Woke up and felt so tired. I want to go back to my family in Fredericksburg, but I have to stay in Florida until my dad returns. My mom keeps me busy day and night. By faith, I will stay focused on what God wants me to do, even though I want to hide and be concerned only with myself.

I hear the front door open, so I go to inspect. I find my mom outside, so I grab her hand and walk with her around the block. As we walk, I think of the following.

> If God said it, I want to believe it.
> If God gives it, I want to receive it.
> If God shows it, I want to perceive it.
> If Satan stole it, I want to retrieve it.

I realized that when I'm giving to someone with no expectation of getting anything in return, I'm acting like my heavenly Father. He will give me what I need as I take care of my mom. Thank you, Lord.

June 1

The story of Elijah is in 1 Kings 17. There was a famine in the land, and God commanded the ravens to feed Elijah by the brook. If we are where God wants us to be, He will take care of us.

I looked at my mom. She was on the couch, falling asleep as she looked through a *Good Housekeeping* magazine. I love her, and God will give me the strength to take care of her. Thank you, Jesus.

Time seems to stop when a crisis in our life happens—it doesn't start again until we say so.

June 3

After all that wonderful Scripture and prayer, I find myself back at square one. *Come on, Sharon!* I felt selfish. I wanted to be alone, but I needed to take care of my mother.

That night, I dressed my mom for bed, took out her dentures, sat her on the bed, and gently laid her down. I pulled the blankets up around her and kissed her forehead. She looked like a sweet, lovely woman. I said a prayer for her, gave her another kiss, and whispered to her, "Please, Mom, when you get to heaven, give Tony a hug for me."

I walked out of her room, closed her door, and put my hands over my face. The image of my son and my mom hugging was overwhelming. Tears streamed down my face. I was glad to be there with my mom. She needed me, and I needed her.

> If you extend your soul to the hungry and satisfy the afflicted soul. Then your light shall dawn in the darkness, and your darkness shall be as the noonday. The LORD will guide you continually,

and satisfy your soul in drought, and strengthen
your bones; you shall be like a watered garden, and
like a spring of water, whose waters do not fail.
(Isaiah 58:10–11)

Thank you, Lord, for guiding me as I care for my mom.

June 8

I can have a very poor self-image due to believing my feelings
and my past instead of what God says in His Word. The way I
choose to view life and grief affects how I relate to those around
me as well as how I relate to my circumstances. I want to live a life
free from all my pain; situations hurt so much because I don't know
how to solve them. You, God, can get me through this path of grief.
I don't know where the path will lead, but I trust I'll be safe as I
travel it. Again I say, "I will be stronger when I get through this
than when I started."

June 17

"And we have known and believed the love that God hath to us.
God is love; and he that dwelled in love dwelled in God and God
in him" (1 John 4:16). How do we love others? We know and rely
on God's love for us. I have to be convinced I am loved totally. It's
a constant; no variations or changing.

We should let people off the hook for not loving us the way we
want them to love us. Only God can love us totally. We can say,
"I can love _____ because God first loved me."
God tells me that He loves me and that I am significant. I can be
so certain of God's love that I am free to love anyone. We have to
put our trust in His love.

June 21

Angie moved in, and everything went well, but I again realize Tony isn't coming home. I so miss my son.

Hurting

I am standing
With my arms outstretched
Where are You?
Where is Your presence?
I need You to find me

—Sharon Capra

I entered my house, and I was very sad. I kept thinking, if only my son could come back for just one more hug or one more smile. Death reminded me of the following scenario: You're sound asleep, and someone suddenly shakes you. Startled, you try hard to open your eyes. "What's going on?" They drag you out of the bed and pull you along the hall to the front door. The door opens, and you're thrust outside. You hear the door slam shut and lock behind you. "Just one more thing I need. I have nothing out here that I need. Please, just one more thing." No one opens the door, and the door can never be reopened.

Death feels that final to me. I am assured in the Word of God that death is not final in eternity's perspective, but on earth, it is final. Tony is in my past and in my future but not in my present. I just keep saying, "Jesus, Jesus," for I know nothing else to say.

I see Tony's children running around the backyard enjoying the beautiful day. How can the same day appear so beautiful to one pair of eyes and so depressing to another pair of eyes? Maybe the only perspective that I should consider is God's perspective; it is a beautiful day regardless of how I feel. Oh my.

June 24

Finally, I climbed out of my pit of despair. It was a place where I had felt safe and cozy, but at the same time, I had such terrible, hidden thoughts. It is easy to get into that pit, but to get out requires a lot of effort. I choose to stay out of that place. Help me, God!

Thought about my life before Tony died. God did equip me for this season. As I thought about all I had done, people I had met, and things God had shown me in His Word, I realized that even if I didn't feel ready to handle this, I was.

Maybe this is how a soldier feels before his first battle. Does he have to reassure himself he's ready? When the sounds of war are blasting around him, there has to be a decision he makes to endure the moment. He's had all the necessary training, and now is the time for him to rely on what he has learned to get him to the other side of this engagement.

Lord, I am trusting You that I can make it right now and every day in the future. You don't leave us unable to get through our daily struggles. We have all we need, and by faith, I will declare, "In Him, I can do all things, including walking this journey of mourning and grief." I will be stronger when I get through this than when I started. I have no idea how long this journey will last, but God has equipped me to get to the other side of it.

June 29

Up and down, up and down … I knew what I was supposed to believe, but my emotions kept going up and down. However, I was determined to keep my eyes on my Savior.

I visited Arlington National Cemetery. My heart started racing, and I became out of breath. I sat in the car and looked at his grave site. The paper marker was gone; in its place was a newly cast tombstone. *No, I cannot go over there. I cannot go over there.* I sat in the car, and still, my heart was racing. I debated whether I should just go home and pretend I'd never went there. *No, I must go. I need to see it.*

I walked over to his grave site and looked at the headstone. There was his name, Anthony Capra, printed on a headstone. No parent should have to look at his or her child's name on a tombstone. All I could do was cry. Someone once said that a good cry can make you feel better, but that cry certainly didn't make me feel better. I knelt down and touched each letter etched on the marker. Oh my.

I didn't want to leave. It was the only place on earth where his body was. I was fully aware my son wasn't there. He was whole, happy, content, and enjoying the presence of God. He wouldn't want to come home and be in that broken body. I knew it was best for him to be in heaven, but I was thinking, *What about me?* I realize it was selfish. I thanked God for taking my son to heaven where there is no pain and no suffering. I was glad Tony was free from any suffering. I got back into my car and drove home. I was quiet and needed time alone.

July 3

When you face your fear, you can become fearless. The whole situation hit me right at the place where I had so much fear. I had twelve children to pray for each day. I went to the task like a honeybee collecting pollen. My fear was that one of those entrusted to me would die. My fear was rooted deeper than I realized. I would do my best to keep my fears hidden so I could prevent them from becoming reality. In fear, I prayed for them all.

I had prayed for Tony, specifically for his safety, and felt reassured. Of course, we should pray for our family's safety, but the motivation behind my prayers was totally fear-driven. This was so eye-opening to me. I was trusting in my prayers, not God's will.

I had worried about what would happen if I didn't pray enough. Or what I would do if he died. I have to trust my Lord to help me. And I have to address that deep-rooted fear. I don't want any fear to be bigger than my faith in God.

As I walked out this new life on the other side of grief, true healing for my mourning began when I started giving to others.

God sent us His Word, and it doesn't return to Him void. The Word of God is the unchaining of the soul for every person with the courage to believe it.

> Now this is the confidence that we have in Him, that if we ask anything according to His will, He hears us. And if we know that He hears us, whatever we ask, we know that we have the petitions that we have asked of Him. (1 John 5:14–15)

I asked for His courage to continue to walk my new life without Tony. God, I know you hear me, and I know it's Your will to help Your children be whole, not broken. Thank you, Lord.

July 4

The whole family went to watch fireworks. We spread out a blanket on the lawn and watched the beautiful sights. Independence Day—we're free from the hold of the enemy. Hallelujah!

July 9

Angie and Rachel, my daughter, went to Florida for the American Legion event. My brother, Paul, was involved with the American Legion Post in the Boca Raton, Florida, area. After they had heard about my son, they offered to sponsor an event to help his family. The legion raised over $30,000 for Angie and my grandchildren. These men and women were so generous.

I watched the five grandchildren while Angie was in Florida, and we had a good time. We watched movies, played outside, swam, and just had fun. My husband and I watched them run across the backyard playing and laughing. It was such a blessing. The littlest, Anna, reminded us of Tony when he was two. At night when I put the younger ones to bed, I would sing the "I Have a Maker" song while I sat next to them on the bed. God is so good!

July 11–12

Angie, her five children, my four youngest girls, and I loaded into the van and headed for Philadelphia for a weekend TAPS event. They sponsor weekends all over the United States, and they offer wonderful programs for the children during that weekend. The children are all excited to spend some time in a hotel, and their enthusiasm was contagious.

As we entered the city, I was apprehensive. What if it bothered the children rather than helped them? I started to pray for them as well as for Angie and myself. *Can we get through this weekend? What feelings will be exposed? Why did we say that we would come?*

TAPS had scheduled events for the children, teens, those who had lost spouses, and those who had lost children. We had our meals in a conference room. During an event for the adults, they wanted everyone to say a fond memory about their loved one. There were about 150 people. I was numb. For some reason, I couldn't remember anything to say about Tony. *What's wrong with me?* I hid behind someone so I wouldn't be called on. I felt so bad that I couldn't speak about my son. I felt ashamed, but I wasn't ready to talk about him. I didn't want to acknowledge to the people in the room that my son was dead. Oh Lord, I love You. Help me!

I went back to my room and cried. I opened my Bible and wrote a poem.

Breathing In Our New Life

We are walking this life together
So let us not fear
What we cannot change
Our paths are set before us all
But we do have a decision
To allow our sadness and grief
To become our reason to not move on

Or to use that sadness to catapult us forward
Only we decide what to do
Each in his own heart
Though each step forward feels big
And picking up our feet seems so heavy
Our hearts yearn to stay
Where the memories of our lost loved one
Are hot and fresh
We must demand of ourselves to take
Our first breathe of our new life
Just like a baby bursting out of the womb
The first moments are uncomfortable
And the breathing feels so unnatural
But eventually just like the newborn
We start to breathe
We start to experience life outside
Of how life was when our loved ones
Were here on earth
But we will always remember
Where we have come from
And whom we have loved
We are blessed by God
To go on and not cursed
We can declare to ourselves
And to those around us
That just because our loved one
Is gone
Our love for them is not
Our love for them will
Challenge us to breathe
In our new future

—Sharon Capra

July 15

Angie, Pastor Ernest, my husband, and I went to Arlington National Cemetery to bury the final remains of my son. They had called Angie to inform her that they had found more remains as they were cleaning up the site. It was a very hard day. Looking at the freshly dug-up ground around his coffin made the situation much worse. How can anyone endure one funeral for a loved one much less two funerals? It just stirred up all the emotions from the first days when we found out and combined them with the sadness and grief up to that moment. I prayed quietly as I questioned God about this. *Why, God? Couldn't you have made sure that all the remains would have been together from the beginning? Why do we have to go through this again?*

We sat facing the small coffin on a pedestal. I closed my eyes and allowed myself to feel the moment. I took a deep breath and concentrated on each inhale and exhale. I thought, *Okay, I can run away from God right now. I can!* I focused on my breathing. *But God, you are the only One who is constant in my life. Everything and everyone changes except You. If I run away from You, I have nothing. No, I have to run to You. I have to. I am hurting so bad. I have to run to my daddy.*

I thought of the verse that when we are weak, He is strong. Yes, we were weak. I asked my husband to pray, and I prayed. I prayed mostly for strength for the coming days, wisdom to know how to respond to those around us, and courage to live again. I thought, *I will be stronger when I get through this than when I started.* I was still clueless about what that meant, but had to say it anyway.

After Pastor Ernest prayed, I walked to the tiny casket. The military funeral department had a piece of masking tape with the name "Capra" on it. I tenderly touched the coffin. How strange it was; I wanted to stay there in that moment for the rest of my life. I allowed myself to take all the time I wanted. I saw Angie and my husband looking at the headstone. My husband wiped off some blades of grass stuck to the headstone. I said, *And yet again will I praise God the maker of heaven and earth.* I made my decision. It was all I knew to do, and it was what I had to do—follow God every day.

I didn't know what that meant, but I knew He was my lifeline to be able to live again.

After the small service, I thought about how fortunate I was to have had two times to say good-bye. I had the big celebration, which I will always treasure, and I had this time as well. It was personal and peaceful, a time set apart from all the busyness to give thanks for Tony's life and to God for one more opportunity to honor my son.

God is not mean. He knew this would happen. I believe God always moves in our lives to make us whole and free. I trust God.

July 21

I am gaining strength in Him daily. I met a young man today who was an EOD army soldier. When I saw the effects of war on him, I started to wonder how my son had dealt with all that he had seen and had had to deal with. War is terrible.

July 23

Suddenly, a new excitement was stirring in my heart. I felt each step I took was easy, and I was smiling at life. I slipped away from all the craziness happening in the house and hid where no one would find me. I opened my Bible and prayed. My grandkids and my younger girls were running around yelling and laughing, and I smiled. We had fourteen people living in our house, and I could see God's hand upon us all. Life is good, Lord.

August 2

We all traveled to California for James's wedding. He had a beautiful wedding on a dinner cruise boat. The boat took off before it started. Tony and I watched the rest of our family take their seats. It was the first time since the funeral that we were all together again. My sons were standing with James, waiting for the bride to come down the aisle. I looked at each of my sons as they anticipated the beginning of the wedding. My hand reached for Tony's, and we looked at each other. How can such great joy and great sadness blend?

We were so delighted to see the beginning of a new couple with all the expectations and dreams they could share, but I was wishing Tony could have been there with us. We all missed him, and being together made us aware of his absence.

It's strange that when someone you love dies, life goes on. This wedding was the first of many events Tony wouldn't be there for. His picture wouldn't be in the wedding album. So strange this thing called death is!

August 10

Life was going on. I checked out ads for school supplies and pulled out my books to get ready for the children's new school year.

August 14

James and his new wife, Tish, visited us for two days. It was such a pleasure to have my family near me. I was so thankful. God, I feel I'm in Your lap, and I'm sure You love me, so I can trust You with my future, aging, and all the changes ahead for me.

August 24

Went to Arlington National Cemetery to see the Run for the Fallen participants. On Flag Day, June 14, 2008 a young man organized friends, family and those interested to run across America. The group called itself Run for the Fallen. Starting at Fort Irwin, California, they ended at Arlington National Cemetery on August 24. They wanted to honor the 4,034 soldiers from all branches of the military who had died in Operation Iraqi Freedom.

They placed an American flag and a sign card in memory of each soldier every mile of the way. It was so emotional as we saw the last runner come into the cemetery. What a tribute! They handed out T-shirts for family members and announced they would like to do this event every year.

September 13

First entry I've made in a while. I hadn't wanted to write my feelings down. I didn't want to remember my journey. I would love it if it weren't true.

My grandson Jared asked me, "What would you do if my daddy came home?" I was surprised at this question from a seven-year-old. I told him I would be very happy because I missed him so much. We smiled. I knew he was thinking the same thoughts as his grandmother.

The Place of Refuge

My mind races
What do I believe?
And Why?
Why did this happen?
Do you still care about me?
I am a floating balloon
Tossed by the breeze
No ability in myself to
Settle down anywhere
Suddenly the Word in me rises
Yet again, will I praise Him
Yet again, will I trust Him
Yet again, will I love Him
And His strength starts to rise within me
And I can live strong
Because He loves me

—Sharon Capra

September 17

Angie called me to ask if I wanted to go with her to Home Depot to pick out appliances for her new house. Every time I saw family members moving forward, I got stuck between being happy for them and sad that Tony wasn't with us. It was fun to see Angie looking for appliances, but I knew Tony would have been delighted to be with his wife looking over all their options.

They had lived in base housing since Tony had enlisted in the Air Force. For Angie, moving into a house not on a base would be a whole new way of life. She had been raised by a mother who was in the military and had never lived outside that way of life.

After we were done shopping, I decided to stay out of the house for the rest of the afternoon. I went to a couple of stores and sat in the parking lot of a fast-food place. Going home meant dealing with all the noise and activity, and I didn't want to be the strong one today. God, give me Your strength.

September 19

Mother Teresa once said, "Like Jesus, we belong to the world—living not for ourselves but for others." She said, "I have found the paradox that if you love until it hurts, there can be no more hurt, only more love" and "A sacrifice to be real must cost, must hurt, and must empty ourselves."

So I thought of a few things after reading what Mother Teresa wrote. When I start to feel negative or overwhelmed with my life, I focus on others. I stay connected with other people. Lift up God; we get happy when He is the center of our lives.

When I went to Florida to take care of my mother, I received a phone call from the American Legion Post in our area. They wanted me to know they had a present for Angie and me. Angie would receive a carved wooden box to place a dedicated Bible in, and I would receive a quilt made by master quilters in the area. As I saw many wonderful gifts and cards come in the mail for Angie,

I was so blessed to see the love of many upon her. But in my heart, I was excited about my quilt, which was a gift for me for the loss of my son. I started to think about it almost daily; I comforted myself with the thought of it.

When I came home from getting groceries, there on the kitchen counter was an opened box. It simply had "Mrs. Capra" on the address label. I peeked inside, and there was the quilt. I glanced at the return label, and sure enough, it was from the master quilters in the area. I pulled back the tissue paper that was holding the quilt and grabbed that wondrous blanket. *Oh my! Here's my quilt.* I called my husband to come look at it. He came, but obviously he didn't share the same thrill I did. I envisioned myself wrapped in my quilt praying in the morning. *Oh happy day! A memento for me!* In the midst of all my joy, my granddaughter came into the room. "Hey Grandma, why do you have mommy's quilt?" Her little voice stopped me in my tracks. I looked at her, folded the quilt, and put it back in the box. I was ready to cry, but I held back the tears. I handed her the box and asked her to take it to her mother.

I quickly walked out of the house and went to a place where I could be alone. Down the long driveway I went, and I started to pick weeds. Pick, cry, pick, cry. *God, all I wanted was that quilt! Why couldn't I have that quilt?* I continued to pick and cry, pick and cry. I heard some young voices calling, "Grandma? Grandma?" I looked up by the house and waved to them but kept crying. I called out to God and finally decided it was just a piece of material, although arranged in a beautiful fashion. I wouldn't allow it to make me miserable, so I walked up the driveway to the house. Dinner needed to be made; my family needed to be fed.

I still wanted that quilt, but I purposed in my mind not to ask Angie for it. I would freely give it to her. I know that sounds silly, but for some reason it meant so much to me. I think it meant so much to me that these women had shown me such kindness by recognizing the loss of my son.

These emotions during grief many times don't make any sense, but they seem to be extremely persuasive. Help me, Lord, to see situations correctly and not through the lens of grief.

October 3

God's Reality

We can believe in Him
Even in our reality of defeat
When all circumstances around
Scream "give up and run from God"
Our emotions and feelings
Agree with the pressure
We don't have to agree with
The situations of this world
Because His truth is bigger
And the only true reality
Stop, oh my mind, stop!
I will change my mind and life
To agree with God over
Whatever I see, think, or feel
You, oh God, have not left me
You, oh God, have not turned away from me
You, oh God, have not tossed me aside
You, oh Lord, love me and encourage me
Through your Word
I am strong in the Lord and in the power of His might

—Sharon Capra

October 5

What highs and lows I've experienced. This week, I was forced to realize that my mom was dying— and basically gone emotionally. I was upset; I wanted everyone to give me an apology—including God. But at the very end of the line of people who owed me an apology should have been Tony. He owed me an apology for dying. My whole life has been changed forever.

But even if everyone stood in line and I got the most encouraging apologies, they wouldn't change how I felt. I wanted my son home. No apology could bring him back.

October 6

I can think and speak like a two-year-old. I felt like saying to God, "You took something of mine! You're a meanie! He's mine!"

What a realization—I was still struggling six months later.

October 8

I read a Scripture in the book of John and inserted my name in it. It was like a light came on inside of me and comforted me. John 14:21 tells me I will love Sharon and manifest myself to Sharon.

I also meditated on Mark 13:14–15 and Luke 24:45. We have to overcome circumstances to be called overcomers. We have a choice to allow our trials to take us away from God or bring us closer to God. Each time we choose to go to God during trials, it makes us stronger and builds us up.

October 10

Helen Keller said, "The most pathetic person in the world is someone who has sight but no vision."

Adversity

When this adversity came
What did I learn about His strength in me?
It is much stronger than any strength I can muster
What did I learn about my weaknesses?
I was so afraid of losing a child.
It made me weak and fearful about losing someone I love
Did I gain anything from this sorrow?
Yes, I learned compassion for others hurting from grief—
New insight into some Scriptures—
New perspective on life and death—
And closer relationships with people

—Sharon Capra

Hopeful people trust God. They are free from the need to be in control. They don't struggle to avoid difficulties. They believe in the goodness of God.

October 17

I tell my soul to hope in God (Psalm 42:11). An Irish proverb says, "Hope is the physician of each misery." The only true hope is the hope we get from God; no other hope will sustain or encourage us.

Angie moved out; she bought a new house about two miles away. The children were so happy running up and down the stairs of their new abode. I was amazed at what God had done for Tony's family. They were starting their new life together. It will never be what it was before, but they can pull together and start new traditions and new experiences.

I drove away from the house and could imagine God saying to me, "Well done! You helped Tony's family, and now it's time for them to learn to begin a new way of life without your son."

I got home and paced. It was hard for me to let them go. When they were living with me, I felt useful; I felt I had a purpose. But they've moved out. I had to find my life and what God wanted me to do with it.

I cried myself to sleep.

October 19

Went to church this morning. I prayed during the service and felt so lonely. At the end of the teaching, the pastor asked if anyone needed prayer. I went up front and asked for prayer. The man who prayed for me gave me Galatians 6:9: "And let us not grow weary while doing good." That meant I could continue to seek God and not become weary in seeking Him. I will continue to come forward for prayer, and I won't stop seeking God. I will be stronger when I get through this than when I started.

October 26

When did I buy into the lie that I could be the perfect parent? When did I try to become all my children's savior? When did I start to feel all my worth on earth was in my children? When did this unreal expectation and vision die? On April 9, 2008.

Blessed are they that mourn for they shall be comforted. Amen. I am comforted by You.

October 27

Pursue Him
And receive
Freedom from fear ruling over me
Freedom from areas of bondage
To my flesh, life can be so very hard. To my spirit, life is easy and full of hope.

November 1

I need to remember three things.

1. Failures should never dominate me. I feel that my son's death was my failure. If I had prayed more, or gotten up earlier, or written him more letters ... But the truth is, it was not my failure. Tony has the victory of a new life in Him. That's not a failure!
2. I have to plan what I want to accomplish in my life. This is so difficult because what I want to do is tread water, and I don't care what plans I have. But God wants me to think again, to dream again, and to live again.
3. I must move forward. This feels like I'm putting Tony in the past. I like to stay where I can clearly remember him. No longer is Tony in my present; he's now in my future! This is God's perspective.

November 3

During a special prayer service at church, I went up front and knelt where Tony's coffin had been during the funeral service. I talked to God while the worship music played. I thought that when the world says a dream ended (the death of a child), God says that's when a dream begins—countless victories, countless salvations, countless deliverances.

What am I going to believe, the world or God? I choose to believe God.

November 6

Went to a retreat in the Shenandoah Mountains. I struggled with the thought of going. I wanted to stay home and not have to face others, but I had a wonderful time with many tremendous women of God. We worshipped the Lord and heard a terrific conference leader. It was good to get my mind off my life and pray for others. It's in giving to others that we find healing for our hearts and minds.

I came home with my heart full of peace. It was great to have had time to meet with God and spend time talking and enjoying so many nice women.

November 30

Been in a struggle lately. I haven't wanted to spend time with the Lord. I can't believe I'm so sad again. I felt I'd made it to the top of a mountain only to fall back into the valley of despair. Lord, help me. I don't want to experience any more hurt, pain, or dying, yet I know that these things will always be around me. I know You hear me. I know You understand me. I know You care for me.

December 7

Read Zephaniah 3:17: "The Lord your God in your midst, the Mighty One. will save; He will rejoice over you with gladness, He will quiet you with His love, He will rejoice over you with singing." What song is He singing over me? I think it's a song of hope, deliverance, protection, and joy.

December 9

Went to Arlington National Cemetery to help lay wreaths at each grave site. We had to get there very early in the morning before all the volunteers came because there would be trouble finding a place to park otherwise.

Morrill Worcester owned a wreath company in Maine. In 1992, He had some surplus wreaths he didn't know what to do with until he remembered his trip to Arlington National Cemetery when he was twelve.

He contacted the cemetery and spoke with a man named James Prout; he owned a trucking company and donated his services to deliver the wreaths. Many groups heard about this and offered their time to lay one at each grave site. This continued until 2005, when Wreaths Across America, a nonprofit, formed. Because of the website pictures and stories, many more people volunteered. On December 13, Congress voted to have a Wreath Across America Day.

I took my son Jake and Tony's oldest son, Mark. It was very cold, and some people were sipping coffee. A truck came up, the door opened, and many big boxes were unloaded. They asked us all to pick up a box and take it to Section 60. The boxes had ten wreaths in each. Someone stood at a designated spot, and each box was opened. We stood in a line and received two wreaths each to put at any grave we wanted. I placed one at Tony's grave. I took a deep breath as I looked at the headstone and his name. Whew!

I went back to the boxes and grabbed two more. I glanced at Tony's grave. His wreath was gone. *Where did it go?* I went over and laid another wreath there. As I walked away, I turned to see that wreath had disappeared too. Finally, it dawned on me that the volunteers were taking the wreaths away because Tony's headstone had a star of David on it and they didn't think it should have a wreath. While living in San Antonio, Tony started going to a Messianic Jewish Temple. He believed that was his heritage through my side of the family. He told me he had researched our eastern European lineage and believed he found a direct family link that established his Judaism. He had the star of David put on his dog tags, and Angie insisted it go on his tombstone. I asked an organizer to tell everyone his family wanted the wreath there.

I looked over the section. It was beautiful covered with all the wreaths, each with a red bow. I met some very nice families of other fallen soldiers. We hung pictures of our loved ones on a small pine. We left around 11:00 a.m. It was a very full day.

December 10

Woke up and continued my early morning prayer time. I'd slacked off for the last few weeks because I felt that if I studied His

Word, I might question it. Yet I was here to stay. I love You, God, with all my heart, soul, strength, and mind.

I questioned my life and my parenting. What did I have to show for my years of parenting? Oh yes. God said, "Only faith, hope, love and the greatest of these is love." That was what I had to show for all these years. God's love was always with me during my days and nights of parenting.

Only You

Only you can know and comfort
Only You can understand
Only You are my daily food for all my life
Only You bring me purpose
Only You

—Sharon Capra

December 11

I looked up "godly meekness" and found a definition I liked: "quiet strength under pressure." It seems possible to have that kind of godly meekness only when the Holy Spirit is leading and guiding me.

I also think that hard times can be like labor pains; I can go through the pain knowing that God will birth something new in my life.

December 22

Went to church. It was decorated with all kinds of beautiful Christmas flowers, trees, and lights. As we started to sing Christmas songs, I had to sit. My heart was so sad. Tony sat next to me. I put my face in his chest and sobbed. I couldn't stop. *This is so hard for me.*

We went to Angie's house. While she went upstairs to put the kids to bed, Tony and I looked at the decorated tree. We listened to "I'll be Home for Christmas." Oh my! One of my grandchildren came downstairs, saw me crying, and hugged me. What a comfort she was!

December 25

We handed out stockings to Sarah, Joe, Jake, Danielle, Joanna, Julia, and Emily. I called my adult children on the phone to wish them a Merry Christmas. All my children will be home for our Capra Christmas by December 28.

We had breakfast and went to Angie's. It was fun to see the grandchildren so happy about their presents. After the presents were opened, we went to Carriage Hill nursing home and sang Christmas carols up and down the halls. It felt so good to be blessing others at Christmas; it took the focus off my son not being here.

We ate a wonderful dinner as a family. I looked at all the family around a big table and smiled, thinking what a great God we have. I was happy to be with my family.

December 28

All my children are home! Well, except for one. I love having everyone home; we get strength from being together. We spent the night talking, laughing, sharing, and wrapping presents. We didn't get to bed until 4:00 a.m.

Our Capra Christmases are fun, game-filled times together. One person (usually the oldest sibling present) is always the master of ceremonies. He organizes the whole event with a few older siblings helping. The planning can sometimes take several days. A few of the older siblings plan games for all to play and give prizes to the winning team. We always have a Capra Trivia game with girls against boys, and that can get wild and crazy.

The younger children woke up and ran into the master bedroom. They piled onto our bed and we said a prayer thanking God for our blessing and for sending His Son, Jesus. We all lined up, youngest to oldest, and ran down the hall to the sunroom while the organizers of this year's special event cheered us along the way.

They ran through streamers, noisemakers blasting, adults clapping, and were sprayed with silly string. We piled into the sunroom, everyone sitting on the couch or the floor. Presents were handed out one at a time; everyone watched and clapped for the receiver of the gift. Because there were twenty-two of us, it took a while to get through even one round of presents.

We had our first game. We went into the kitchen, where plates were lined up on the counter. On each plate were big bubble gum balls covered with Cool Whip. Each person had to put his or her face in the Cool Whip and find the bubble gum. Once they found each piece, they had to chew it and then try to make a person's shape with it. Then the master of ceremonies decided who won the round by deciding which person-shaped gum figure he liked best. We also played a game drinking soda with a straw.

I made a big dinner, and we had a family soccer game outside. It was a fun day, but I thought of Tony and wished he were with us.

January 1

I didn't stay up for the New Year. I retreated to my bed before 11:00 p.m. It all seems so different, not getting a phone call from Tony. He always wanted to be the first one to call. He was so competitive! We gathered in the sunroom to get a family picture. I had one taken with my five sons and me. We posed and made some silly faces, but it just wasn't the same without Tony.

My husband made a nice, big dinner, and we all sat around until the football game came on. What will this new year be like? I need to get an attitude of hope for this year—hope for living and not just existing. Oh Lord, I need You!

January 5

Every day is cold and dreary. I thought of Tony. I grabbed my coat and keys and drove to Arlington National Cemetery. The wreaths were still at each grave site. The snow and the wreaths looked awesome. I was the only one visiting, and I felt so alone. I walked to his tombstone and was amazed I wasn't crying. Then the tears come. I held my mitten-covered hands to my face and thought, *I'm going to be stronger when I get through this than when I started.* Where was this journey taking me? Sometimes, I felt I knew, but other times, I had no clue. How would I know when I'd made it to the end of my grieving?

I stared at the gravestones. *How do I find such comfort in coming here?* I knew Tony wasn't there, but I felt such comfort in being there.

I started the car and let the heat warm me up. I wasn't ready to leave. *What are you doing right now, Tony?* Slowly I started moving and headed home. I really missed him.

February 17

Traveled with Joanna to see my son, Jason, and his wife, Tricia. Tricia was pregnant with their third child, and we were going there to help out.

Joanna is so good with little children; they just love her. It was fun for me to have time alone with Joanna. This whole situation with my son dying has made me super aware of my other children. I try to make time for each one and breathe in the everyday moments of life.

February 18–19

Arrived at Jason and Tricia's house. Jason was in the Air Force and going through his anesthesiology residency. I spent the day enjoying my precious granddaughters, Kristin and Katie. Jason was out of town at a physician's conference; Tricia was having contractions all day. Just after she put the girls to bed, her water broke. She called Jason, but there was no way he could make it back in time.

I grabbed her hands, and we prayed. All I could think of was that God loved Tricia and would provide just what she needed to get through her labor and delivery. It was perfect timing that I had arrived when I had. Her water had broken at 10:00 p.m., so we went to the hospital. She labored for a short while, and when they examined her, she was already nine centimeters. I thanked God for such a quick and easy labor and delivery.

Caleb Anthony was born at 12:30 a.m. on February 19. What a cute baby! And Tricia did a great job. I was so blessed to see new life come into this world. It was awesome. Thank you, Lord. When I saw Jason hold his son for the first time, I cried. Tony would have loved to have seen this new little guy. God bless you, my little grandson.

February 27

It's been fun spending time with Jason's family. We decided to rent a movie for the night, and we needed snacks, so I volunteered to run to the store on base to pick up a few things.

Katie was getting tired, so I asked Tricia if I could take her for a ride. I got her coat on and put her in her car seat. I was driving Tricia's car, and she had a CD in the player. We listened to "You Raise Me Up" by Josh Groban. I felt so connected to the song that I played it again. I parked at the store. Tears rolled down my cheeks as I listened to the words. My granddaughter sat happily in her car seat while I was total mess sobbing. *Will I ever get over this pain?*

March 14

Tony's Birthday. Woke up and wanted to feel sorry for myself. It was a cold, rainy, dreary day. A perfect day to mope around. But I could take only an hour of my stupid pity party. I had to pray and ask God to help me. I felt hopeless whenever I allowed myself to be depressed.

Angie called; she wanted to go to the cemetery with all the grandchildren. My four youngest girls—Danielle, Joanna, Julia, and Emily—came also. My husband was at work in DC, so he drove over there to meet us. Angie picked us up, and we went to get flowers. I like to put white roses at his grave as that brings me back to when I had Tony.

We bought cupcakes too. We drove up together. When we got there, we walked to his grave. Angie and I cut the flowers, and Tori and Julia went to get the flower holders. When they got back, we put our flowers in the holders, and I taped a card from the girls on the headstone.

We took many group pictures to put on Facebook. We circled Tony's grave and held hands. I said a prayer of thanksgiving for his life and how grateful we were for him. I cried as I prayed. It was so hard to get through the day. Angie handed cupcakes to each of us, and we sang "Happy Birthday" to Tony. I walked to my husband and cried. He held me tight. I could tell he was holding back tears. I didn't want to leave Arlington; it always felt good to be there.

When I had to go home, I felt empty inside. *I will be stronger when I get through this than when I started.* I still didn't know what that meant, but I felt His comfort when I thought it.

March 28

Angie and Tony's wedding anniversary. I called her up, and we decided to go to Arlington National Cemetery and have lunch afterward. It was good to be together. His birthday was such a hard day for me, but it must have been so difficult for her.

We had a wonderful lunch and talked about many things. I'm so thankful for Angie. God, thank you for bringing her into my son's and my life. I have been so blessed.

April 3

I had to take my car to the dealership for repairs. I started talking to the salesman about Tony. It seemed important to me to talk about Tony. I'd pour out stories about him to any breathing creature. *Why am I doing this? He doesn't even know me or care about me.*

That evening, my church sponsored a community event, Awaken the Dawn. Many people came from all over, and they had anointed speakers. One spoke about sonship, and I took notes. I have always known that I was a child of God, but the way he presented the message stirred my heart. Maybe that was why I felt compelled to mention my son to the salesman. I needed to let others know he was still my son and would always be. He didn't lose that position because he had died.

We as well don't lose that position with God. He is our Father, and I wondered, *Does He talk about us?*

April 9: One-Year Anniversary

A year later—the anniversary of my son's death. I realize that though I'll always miss Tony, I don't have to hurt each time I think of him. I can start to breathe again and not feel guilty about it. It's time for me to get up.

I Am Here

I am here—grief tried to destroy me but clearly it did not
By faith in the living God
I acknowledge Tony's going home is a victory
It is the victory of eternal life over death
that gives our life meaning.
We can be free—free to care, give and love others
because we have no fear of our future
and we will all be gathered in heaven one day
Tony's going home is also a celebration

A celebration of the providence of our heavenly Father
and of God's hand bringing my son home
God was faithful and immediately
embraced his new reborn son into heaven
"Look," He says to all those in heaven.
"Look! My son Tony is home!"
And death causes us to take notice of the
everyday wonders of life—
the smiles and the little things done between loved ones
So we can celebrate those moments also
Tony's going home is also a commemoration—
to be recalled and remembered for years to come
God gave us more than we knew that day
He led us to a new way of living.
No fear in death and that there are some things
that are meant to live on in our hearts
and that is our love for Tony,
our memories together, the laughter and gifts we shared
And some things are meant to die—our
regrets, our mistakes, and anger
No one is born brave
From the first days of our life we can get scared;
loud noises, being moved quickly and so many more things
We feel like we cannot possibly be brave enough for certain events
Yet God calls us to be brave
But how? By trusting in Him above the grief, pain and loss
—choosing to deny your thoughts of incredible force
to say even though I am so sad I will believe God
His Word says,
"In the day when I cried out, You answered me
And made me bold with strength
In my soul." (Psalm 138:3)

—Sharon Capra

Lord, it's been an incredible year of unbelievable highs and lows. I've fallen into despair and saw the slimy pit of depression try to grab me, and I've risen to heavenly places where I thought my heart would never stop singing. But no matter how many times I was emotionally low or high, You remained constant. Thank You, Lord, for You showed me You are Jehovah, the unchanging One, and I am stronger now than I was a year ago.

CHAPTER 3

Definition of Grief

We were created to care about and love people. I'm sure this was God-given so we can form relationships, bless others, and in turn be blessed. Naturally, we form attachments to those we care for. When someone we love passes away, we experience many emotions.

But what is grief? Why does it consume us? Why does it manifest itself in so many ways? Because we are all distinct, we respond to people and situations in unique ways. Each relationship we have is different. We could have known others all our lives, maybe even depended on them for their provision for us, or we could have known them only slightly. In the end, though, we will go through each loss in our own way and shouldn't compare or judge one another's reactions.

Our past is filled with connections and memories of all the people we have encountered. When others die, we focus on what their lives meant to us. Maybe we remember the first time we met them or how they were always in our lives. Memories flood our minds, and it makes us sad to know we won't have any more time with them.

We feel a strong sense of loss when they're missing from our family pictures or when we're unable to call them. It's sad to think about how they will miss all our families' life events—birthdays, weddings, graduations, Thanksgivings, Christmases, and anniversaries. Each day brings multiple experiences we'll be unable to share with them. Sometimes, we may miss the sound of their voices, their laughs, or even their smells.

When someone dies, we can also have the loss for the days ahead. Proverbs 31:25b (NIV) says, "She can laugh at the days to come." From the perspective of loss, we could say to ourselves, *Why laugh? My life is no longer the same without my loved one.* Discouragement can creep into our thoughts. We Christians know God has provided a remedy for our discouragement. We can smile at the future not because they will come back to join us but because one day we will join them. I believe we will always have a desire to see them again. But with Jesus dwelling in us, we can acknowledge our loss and always hope for tomorrow.

There are different types of loss, and each can be difficult; we can't say one type is greater than another. Grief is a personal journey and cannot be compared others' grief.

Loss of a Child

When we lose a child, we might feel a part of who we are is gone. Taking family pictures can make us feel there's someone missing in the photo. This loss can take on many different struggles as we move forward in life.

Loss of a Spouse

We can experience loneliness and miss the comfort and companionship only a spouse can bring. Those whose marriages were also friendships will experience the double loss of spouses and best friends. People can also worry about their financial situations after a loss; that can affect their daily living situations as well.

Loss of a Sibling

A sibling could be a vital connection to your childhood; that sibling may have always been there for you. You may have many fun memories of that sibling. Or maybe you could never seem to connect with him or her and now feel guilty about that.

Loss of a Father

Your father may have been the first male person in your life. He was the one meant to provide for you and help protect you. So many strong emotions could surface depending on what kind of relationship you had with your father.

Loss of a Mother

The emotional connection you had with your mothers might make her loss particularly hard. Your mother may have always wanted the best for you; maybe, she was never there for you. Either way, you can still feel like a lost child in a big crowd when your mother passes away.

Loss of a Friend

A close friend can be a confidante, a person you had daily conversations and built memories with. These wonderful experiences can make you miss your friend very much.

Loss Due to Suicide

This can be a complicated, traumatic grieving situation. Someone's suicide can blindside those who loved that person. It can also create a lot of guilt if there were some danger signs the person exhibited that you ignored. Many unanswered questions can provoke endless conversations among those left behind.

In addition, shame can rear its ugly head when you have to inform others about a loved one who committed suicide. These thoughts can layer themselves on top of the grieving process. The act of suicide shouldn't consume you to the degree that you cannot reflect on the life the person lived and how much you loved him or her. Seek professional help if you are too overwhelmed to deal with this loss as well as any other.

Loss Due to Murder

This can also make for another complicated grieving scenario, one that can give us a strong sense of loss of control for not having saved a loved one. We may ask ourselves, *Why couldn't I protect them?* This can throw us into a helpless state. Even though my son was in the military and I was aware of the possibility he could lose his life, I felt this type of loss and had to seek God for His help.

Whatever our loss, it can stop our lives for a season, sometimes longer. That time can take every ounce of focus we have.

Seek God's help so you can literally live in His strength to get through it.

CHAPTER 4

Death Can Wound the Heart

When we receive the devastating news that someone we love has died, we can feel wounded in our hearts. Even though God has provided a way for us to heal these wounds, we can find ourselves entangled in them. We are aware that death is a part of our life on earth. Every year, an estimated two million die in the United States. But when it happens to us, we can harbor two wounds from experiencing grief—anger and the inability to forgive.

Anger can rise up in our reaction to the loss. It's a natural response to a negative situation that has happened to us, and we can feel we have a right to respond to the situation in anger. In our culture, we observe people receiving retribution from those who hurt them; our courts are full of such cases. Sometimes, even if we get back our property, money, or other possessions, it doesn't totally soothe our hearts. At times, it's impossible to get back what was taken (for instance, when someone we love has died).

Regardless of how their lives ended, the question of who is to blame can cause anger and bitterness to rise up in our hearts. We can experience lifelong inner turmoil and grief from this conflict. We want our loved one back; we feel we've been wronged. Only God's peace will bring us complete healing from this.

Shalom is a Hebrew word for peace—complete or full peace. It also means to have well-being and tranquility. This greeting could be given when someone is coming or going. What a great reminder to hear every day. God's peace means that nothing is missing or broken. Shalom can be our declaration, especially in times of grief.

Unforgiveness is the second weapon the enemy uses to wound us during our grief. We can be unforgiving toward our departed loved one for leaving us, or toward the medical profession for not doing enough, or toward others if they caused the death. It can seem unfair and impossible to forgive. We feel the pain of loss and anguish at the thought that those who caused our loss get to go free.

Sometimes when there has been sickness or a sudden loss, we have to forgive God for the situation we are in. This reminds me of a story of how the Romans were supposed to have inflicted one particular punishment. It's a great illustration of what we do to ourselves when we refuse to forgive. They would strap a dead person to the back of a prisoner. As the deceased body decayed, the prisoner's body would also start to decay where their flesh met. Eventually, the prisoner would die from being in contact with rotting flesh.

We experience something similar when we carry unforgiveness on our backs; it can destroy us. The problem with carrying these twin wounds is that the relief doesn't last. It only masks the pain. Our brain starts to connect a false sense of relief with these bad feelings, so we feel unable to move on. A behavior that starts as an attempt to make us feel in control can end up controlling us.

Anger and unforgiveness can progress from sharp emotions in the grieving process to a devouring, debilitating lifestyle. So why do we hold onto them? We feel too hurt or too overwhelmed to forgive. We can also derive a sense of power by holding onto anger and unforgiveness. Our right to be angry and not want to forgive provides us some comfort. But when we hold onto anger and unforgiveness, we stop coping with our healing. These thoughts can consume us until we haven't the desire to move on. Therein lies the problem.

God tells us He heals the brokenhearted. Healing begins with a decision; it isn't forced on us. We have to want it and ask for it. We need the Holy Spirit to help us, and that requires us to pray for His help.

> Therefore I take pleasure in infirmities, in reproaches, in needs, in persecutions, in distresses for Christ's sake. For when I am weak, then I am strong. (2 Corinthians 12:10)

Forgiveness and letting go of anger might not be a single experience but a process. Let's look at the life of Corrie ten Boom, who had many reasons to be angry and unforgiving but found peace in trusting God and His ways to achieve freedom from these twin death wounds.

Corrie and her sister were sent to a concentration camp during World War II for hiding Jews in their home. Corrie's sister didn't survive the harsh treatment and horrific conditions in the camp. Having a hard time letting go of her anger, Corrie had to ask God to help her forgive those who had been so cruel to her and her sister. After Corrie was released, she had many opportunities to share her experiences and forgiveness.

After the war, when she was speaking at a prayer meeting, she recognized someone in the crowd—one of the guards from the camp. After Corrie concluded her message, the former guard came up to her and explained he was at that point a Christian. He claimed he had asked God to forgive the cruel things he had done. After hearing Corrie's message, he asked her if she could forgive him. He stretched out his hand to Corrie. She thought of her sister. She looked at his outstretched hand and hesitated to shake it. Anger enveloped her.

She knew that forgiveness was an act of the will and that she couldn't forgive him without the help of Jesus. She said a prayer asking Jesus to help her. It was a simple but powerful prayer. She stretched her hand toward the former guard; she trusted in Jesus' help to supply the feeling of forgiving this man.

She wrote later that something truly amazing happened to her as she allowed herself to respond to this young man. Corrie said that love—real love—had poured out of her for the man. It was a love that could have come only from God. She felt released from the anger she and for him and could then really forgive him.

Here's another dramatic story of forgiveness. The whole world heard about the story of a small group of Amish who forgave one person who caused the death of five of their young family members. On October 2, 2006, in a small, one-room Amish schoolhouse in West Nickel Mines, Pennsylvania, a delivery man named Charles Roberts walked in. He wanted to kill himself and others. He had been struggling with many personal issues and somehow felt this was a way to stop those torturous thoughts.

A woman he released ran to get help, but within thirty-two minutes, the episode was over. Five young students, including two sisters from one family, were killed. Reports of the Amish community's forgiveness of the killer sent shock waves throughout the world. How could they forgive so quickly? Didn't they understand? Were they in grief and didn't realize the totality of this crime?

Letters of support and comfort poured in from all over the world to the families. Money poured in as well to help the families who had lost loved ones. The Amish donated much of what was sent to them to the killer's wife. Charles Roberts was buried a day after one of the murdered girls was, and some of the Amish congregation went to the cemetery to show their compassion for the widow.

I heard of a man who had been invited to attend the funeral of one of the Amish girls. The Amish held funeral services for their loved ones in their homes. Only rarely had someone from the outside of their community been invited into an Amish home. This man remarked that he could sense the deep love this family had for their precious young girl. She was laid out on one of the dining room tables in her traditional Amish outfit. People were speaking quietly to one another. Frequently, the mother would walk up to the table, look at her daughter, and adjust the young girl's bonnet or dress.

These were mothers and fathers who cared deeply for their children but somehow knew they had to forgive. How could anyone who had been affected by such a horrendous crime forgive? It was only through our Lord. We will still feel the pain of the loss and the longing to see our loved ones again, but forgiveness gives us the ability to breathe again.

No matter how we feel, we can choose to let go of anger and unforgiveness by the power of the Holy Spirit and render those two forces powerless in our lives. When we make that choice, God will accomplish in our lives what only He can accomplish. He can give us wholeness and healing.

We don't have to remain broken and wounded all the days of our lives unless we decide that is how we want to live. Deuteronomy 30:19 (NIV) tells us, "Now choose life so that you and your children may live."

CHAPTER 5

Old Testament Wisdom for Those Who Grieve

In 2 Samuel, David had relations with Bathsheba—not his wife—and she conceived. After the child was born, he became very sick, and David sought God to spare the child. He fasted and lay all night on the ground.

The elders of his household stood beside him to raise him from the ground, but he was unwilling and wouldn't eat with them. On the seventh day, the child died. David's servants were afraid to tell him that the child was dead; they said, "Behold, while the child was still alive, we spoke to him, and he didn't listen to us. How then can we tell him that the child is dead, since he might do himself harm?" However, David rose, washed, anointed himself, and changed his clothes, and he came into the house of the Lord and worshipped. Then he came to his own house, and when he requested it, they set food before him.

This passage illustrates the emotional and physical trauma David experienced at the death of his child.

1. feelings of devastations
2. a comprehension of the finality of death

3. preoccupation with regret
4. inability to think clearly
5. being awash with sorrow
6. doubting God
7. personal physical disregard

When we go through the first days, months, and years of grief, we can move back and forth between these stages in no order, but that's normal. The stages aren't steps in a process we follow to reach an end. Sometimes in the morning, I felt strong and able to handle the day, but by the afternoon, I was crying and sad. This is typical for those going through this challenging, life-changing event. But even in the midst of our pain and our saddest day, God provides help in many different ways but especially through His Word.

As Christians, we should have hope that one day we will get past these stages and start to live again, not the same as before the death of our loved one, but living with the knowledge that God will continue to care for our loved ones in heaven and will help us through our time on earth. We can anticipate our joyful reunions with our loved ones in the future. Hallelujah!

Let's see if we can apply the Word of God to understanding our personal process of mourning. We'll look closer at the stages David went through in working through his grief.

1. David Lay on the Ground

The news of his son's illness literally drove David to the ground in prayer and supplication. In some cases such as David's, our loved one is hanging between life and death; at other times, our loved is suddenly gone, and we're in shock. We fall to the ground in either case. Everything appears to be crashing around us, especially in the first few days.

Our confrontation with death forces us to stay for a time on the ground. We have suffered the greatest loss known to humanity—the loss of a loved one. We are shocked, dazed, confused, devastated, and unable to think clearly. We feel overcome by a strong wave we cannot stand up against. We will be deeply affected. We may have trouble sleeping, thinking clearly, or functioning. But that's a normal response to death.

God designed us to love. When we lose someone close, we will grieve. There is not a programmed process for getting through our loss, but we can find help in God.

If you find you are unable to move from the ground or it has been longer than six months, it's time to find help. Experienced Christian therapists and counselors can help you in your grieving and can be wonderful sources of comfort. They can lead you to God, and you can experience His love. That's exactly what you need at that time.

People helping us are a tremendous blessing, and we need them when we are grieving. But remember, they can never totally deliver us from our pain—only God can. We might find it easy to make someone else responsible for delivering us from mourning, but if we insist that others are to be our saviors, we can be disappointed.

Let God be your God even if you don't understand everything, even if you don't know how God will do it, even if you're a new believer, even if you're scared, or even if you're angry at the situation. He is the only One who can totally deliver us. A good counselor or someone you love and trust will point you to our Lord and Savior.

One of the helpful resources that I found at that time was an organization called GriefShare. The organization hosts meetings all over the United States and Canada and other countries. All are welcome regardless of whether they go to church. They usually meet in churches and offer videos, workbooks, and time to share. The seminars last thirteen weeks, but you can join anytime. I cried almost the whole time during my first meeting, but I felt free to do that. It was a blessing to me, and I highly recommend it.

> I am weary with my groaning; all night I make
> my bed swim; I drench my couch with my tears.
> (Psalm 6:6)

How long we stay on the ground depends on us, no one else. I fell to the ground when I heard the news. My feet wouldn't hold me. It was as if someone had pulled a rug out from under me. I didn't want to get up. I thought if I moved from that spot, I'd have to face this incredible pain and start to function in everyday life.

As in all situations in life, I found reading the Bible was a great comfort and source of healing. In Psalm 37:24, we read, "Though he fall, he shall not be utterly cast down; For the Lord upholds him with His hand." This verse really ministered to me, and I confessed it and thought of His hand reaching out to me.

2. David Rose from the Ground

When King David heard his child had died, he rose from the ground. His beloved child was gone, and he recognized death for what it was. According to my interpretation of this Scripture, David seemed to rise up quickly and have control of his emotions, but when his son Absalom died, he responded quite differently. In 2 Samuel, when David heard about his son being killed, he cried out, "My son, my son" in total grief.

John 19:25 mentions that Mary couldn't stay away from seeing her Son on the cross. What a horrible image that was for her, and yet she was there. Her love for Jesus made her stay. She witnessed his death knowing there was nothing she could do to stop what her Son was going through. All she could do was face the reality of His dying.

For most of us, that's the time when our loss of a loved one sinks in. We might ask ourselves, *Can I survive without him? Why did she die? Could their deaths have been avoided?* We can ask the same questions repeatedly but find no answers. That's the time when we count the cost of this experience, evaluate it, and meditate on it.

Death is unnatural to us. How can we feel at that point? We may want empathy and try to make others give it to us only to realize that no one can give us what we need. Or we may want sympathy. I remember wanting everyone to know what I had just gone through.

I would tell strangers or store clerks or my dentist or whoever happened to look my way. After I did that, I would wonder why I had opened my mouth. I wanted someone to join me, to understand me, but that didn't make me feel any better. I started to experience anxiety, fear, worry, loneliness, and despair.

James 1:2 states, "My brethren, count it all joy when you fall into various trials." But how can we consider this a time of joy? Grief is a trial; to count it all joy seems to be humanly impossible!

As I was pondering this verse, I watched the 1952 version of *Titanic* on TV. As the ship started to sink, crew members shouted at the wealthy passengers to put on life jackets. The movie showed a small group of passengers standing motionless. The situation was dire. They could put on life jackets or stare at their impending doom.

Joy is our life jacket for every situation, even our most overwhelming ones. We believers can choose to put it on or not. The Word of God cries out to us, "Count it all joy whenever you encounter various trials, knowing that the testing of your faith produces patience. But let patience have its perfect work, that you may be perfect and complete lacking nothing."

We can let our situation overwhelm us, or we can find joy in Him. The water we find ourselves in may be turbulent, but we can always say, "I have a Savior who is with me in this trial, and in that I find joy. He will help me in the testing of my faith, and He will develop patience in me. I will lack nothing of what I need to get through this loss."

I don't believe the verses are saying we should be joyful for the grieving and loss but that even in the midst of our loss, Jesus is with us. He will carry us when we cannot go on. He will never leave us. I remember thinking that everything in my life was changing except for my Lord and Savior. His constancy brought me joy and comfort. As the Scriptures tell us, "The joy of the Lord is our strength"

In Matthew 5:4, we read, "Blessed are those who mourn, for they shall be comforted." During that time, I thought of children running to their parents to be comforted after they had gotten hurt. Sometimes, I would think of Jesus just holding me and comforting me.

3. David Washed

We can wash ourselves from regrets and feeling brokenhearted.

> Lord, all my desire is before You; And my sighing is not hidden From You. My heart pants, my strength fails me; As for the light of my eyes, It also has gone from me. (Psalm 38:9–10)

In Judges 16:21, we read that Samson, after he was blinded and put in chains, was forced to move a grinding stone over and over. This reminds me of how we can feel helpless and bound by our regrets and brokenhearted thoughts that keep repeating in our minds.

Regrets can cause us constant sadness. We all have moments of sadness, but regrets can permeate every thought we have and affect our actions. Looking back at the relationship we had with our loved one, we can regret how we acted with them or maybe what we didn't do with them. We can replay those moments and feel even more regret. We recognize we have no more time to spend with them. So how do we handle these regrets? Do we let these regrets control our thoughts and our lives? We may never forget individual regrets, but how do we respond to them?

As children of God, we must learn to let go of our regrets. Philippians 3:13 (ESV) tells us,

> I do not consider that I have made it my own, but one thing I do; forgetting what lies behind and straining forward to what lies ahead I press on toward the goal for the prize of the upward of God in Christ Jesus.

In some situations, we may need to get help to help us address particular regrets. Please seek the help you need.

I define being brokenhearted as a distressing psychological state that includes feelings of helplessness, anguish, remorse, pain, and loss of control. We can be prone to isolating ourselves when we feel this way. Feelings of self-destruction and hopelessness can permeate our thinking. When in this state, we don't want to seek help; we want to turn inward. We can find ourselves overwhelmed and hopeless. There seems to be no reason to live on without our loved one.

One of the many blessings God gave us through His Son is release from being brokenhearted. In Psalm 147:3, we read, "He heals the brokenhearted and binds up their wounds," and in Luke 4:18–19, Jesus said, "The Spirit of the Lord is upon Me, because he has anointed Me to preach the gospel to the poor. He has sent Me to heal the brokenhearted." We can be free from expressing our grief in self-destructive ways when we believe and accept what Jesus did for us.

I remember coming back from church one Sunday. The church service had been uplifting, and everyone but me seemed to have been smiling. It was a beautiful summer day, but I was in an internal storm. *Why do I feel so miserable?* I drove home in silence. As I entered the house, I let out a big sigh—I was brokenhearted, and my negative thoughts were inviting me to dwell in a state of hopelessness. I could feel the heaviness of it, but I wanted to stay there.

Then I saw in my mind's eye a big whirlpool in the middle of the room. It looked so inviting, warm, and secure. It was a pit of despair calling to me, "Sharon, come on! Jump into this pit. It is where you can hide and escape the pain of grief." I wanted to jump in and fall down the hole, but I thought that if I did, I'd have a hard time getting out. I had to resist the temptation. All I could say was, "Jesus, Jesus, Jesus!" I let the name of Jesus wash over me and felt the brokenhearted emotions flow off. I kept confessing that Jesus healed my broken heart and bound my wounds.

Proverbs 15:13–14 (Amplified) tell us, "But by sorrow of heart the spirit is broken." We can allow sorrow to invade our hearts and break our spirits. We can tell ourselves it doesn't matter if we stay in that state, but it matters to God, to those around us, and to the memory of our loved ones.

On the other hand, the pain we experience can be a very useful indicator that we need help. Usually when we are in pain, we reach out. If we are injured or hurt, we seek out someone to help us. Pain is a signal that we need help. God puts people in our path to help us because He wants us to be cared for in our time of grief.

Be strong and brave enough to let yourself grieve. God will provide what you need. He doesn't want you to be full of regrets or be brokenhearted, but He knows you'll have to go through the pain of your loss.

4. David Anointed Himself

At times during our grief, we feel unable to think in an orderly way. Our minds can become befuddled, and that can be disarming. When the disciples were being tossed to and fro in a storm at sea, they were unable to stop the storm. But we don't have to rely on our own strength. Praise God!

We can use God's Word to anoint ourselves and override our feelings and emotions. We can dwell on what we have or don't have. But through praying in the Spirit and praying His Word, we can find His strength to overcome and settle the storm within us. Isaiah 26:3 tells us that the Lord will keep us in peace as we keep our minds on Him. And at that time, we need His peace, which will stabilize our minds, thoughts, and emotions.

We can see God's Word hold up under our trials; He wants us to see His Word working in our lives. Scripture demonstrates the power and faithfulness of our God. Luke 8:21 tells us that those who hear and do the Word of God are considered Jesus' mother and brothers. As His family, we can have whatever He has provided for us.

When my children and grandchildren come to our dinner table, they are encouraged to have whatever has been prepared for them. So too, God has called us His children, and He delights in our seeking Him through His Word.

Hearing the Word is only half of what we need to do; we must also do the Word. To me, that means I can speak Scriptures over my life, my trials, and my sorrow. Isaiah 55:11 declares that the Word will not return void; rather, it will accomplish what He pleases and will prosper in the thing for which He sent it. I found many Scriptures that helped me during my grief, including Romans 15:13, Psalm 23, 1 Thessalonians 4:13–18, Psalm 4:8, Philippians 4:13, and 1 Peter 5:7.

Write down what you're going through and take it before the Lord. If a verse or a thought comes to you during prayer, write it down next to what you wrote. It can be a comfort to see those Scriptures or inspirational words as you pray and talk to God.

5. David Changed Clothes

We can take off our clothes of hopelessness and put on garments of hope. John 11 relates the story of Jesus going to Bethany because Lazarus, a friend, had died. Lazarus's sisters were very upset, and He went to comfort them. His compassion for the situation was recorded in verse 35: "Jesus wept." We are also that valuable to him. Lazarus was already laid to rest and wrapped in common burial clothes. Jesus stood in front of the tomb and cried out, "Lazarus, come forth." Suddenly, out from the tomb Lazarus came, still bound up. Jesus said, "Loose him, and let him go."

Sometimes, we who are left behind can put on the clothes of death and feel bound in despair and limited in everyday activities. I feel Jesus is crying out to us, "Loose them and let them go." We can be released only by our God. Praise His holy name. When we don't seek to stop our pain, sadness, sorrow, and grief, we can stop noticing the moments we're living. We can become satisfied to stay right where we are. We are, in essence, wearing our grief.

Because my husband and first four sons were in the Air Force, I felt at home on military bases. After Tony died, I'd go to the closest base to go to the commissary. I would look at all the men and women in uniform and wonder if they could see I was in mourning. I thought surely they must have known one of their comrades has fallen. Couldn't they see it when they saw me? I was wearing it, right? Wasn't it obvious? But in truth, no one would seem to notice me, and I would leave more consumed in my thoughts than before.

You will miss so many wonderful, daily events if hopelessness fills your mind. You have the choice to take off your clothes of grief. Next time you're hurting from your grief, try to clear your mind and look at the moment you're in. Life offers you many amazing blessings. Your hopelessness can fall off, and hope can begin to grow in you.

Another way we can find hope is through the people God puts in our path. If we were on a sinking ship, we'd look around for the strongest swimmer or the most confident person to help us. So too, in times of this kind of crisis, when we are in the unknown sea of mourning, we can and must look for the strength God offers us. God has placed remarkable, compassionate brothers and sisters in the faith in our paths who can pray with us and give us words of comfort. They will direct us to the Lord of all comfort while they pray with and support us.

My friend and sister in the Lord, Lauren, came to my mind shortly after the funeral. I called her, and she welcomed me over. I allowed myself to look to someone else for help. We talked, shared, and prayed together. It was such a blessing. Her God-given strength was so calming and reassuring that I was able to go on even if it was for just one more day. God placed many people right when and where I needed them. He has done the same for you.

> The Lord is good to those who wait for Him. To the soul who seeks Him. (Lamentations 3:25)

It's good to hope and wait quietly for the salvation of the Lord. You can also find hope for your life through the plans God has for you. Picture you and God sitting on the steps of a big, Southern house with a wonderful wraparound porch. He has His arm around your shoulders, and you're both looking at a big field in front of the house. Think of the field as your future. Behind you is the house with a closed door. It represents the past, which cannot happen again. But you have the present; God is by your side, and the future is before you. God reminds you in Jeremiah 29:11: "For I know the thoughts that I think toward you, says the Lord, thoughts of peace and not of evil, to give you a future and a hope." He gently says, "I will stay with you every day, and I have a future and a hope laid out before you. And my hope will not disappoint."

6. David Worshipped

In 1 John 4:16, we read, "And so we know and rely on the love that God has for us." Can we know how much God loves us? Can we put our trust in His love? We can when we worship Him in the midst of our pain.

Naomi was a woman in the Old Testament book of Ruth. While living in Moab, Naomi lost her husband and two married sons. In grief, she was going back home to Bethlehem. When she arrived, some people there recognized her. She told them to call her Mara, meaning "bitter," not Naomi. She felt that the Almighty had dealt very bitterly with her and that she had no reason to be happy. We can understand this; it can distract us from worship.

Worship? How can we worship God when we're in such pain? It makes it difficult for us to focus on anything. I was enabled to worship God when I looked to these Scriptures for His help and decided to believe His Word rather than what I felt. It brought such peace back into my heart.

- Hebrews 12:2 (NIV): Let us fix our eyes on Jesus, the author and perfecter of our faith.

79

- Isaiah 45:22 (NIV): Turn to me and be saved, all you ends of the earth; for I am God, and there is no other.
- Psalm 73:28 (NIV): But as for me, it is good to be near God. I have made the Sovereign LORD my refuge; I will tell of all your deeds.

I challenge you to let go of questions about how or why you should worship because God is exactly who you need when you're in pain. Find a Christian song to listen to, go for a walk in the beautiful outdoors, hide in your room with the Bible, attend a church or Bible study where God's love is preached—whatever you need to let yourself fall into your heavenly Father's arms.

The first time I went to church after Tony had died, I listened to the songs of worship rise. As I rested in the music, I was comforted and found peace. I didn't sing or make any movements; I just listened and relaxed. Many times, we can run from God in a crisis instead of running to Him. I found myself running to Him with all my heart.

> Oh come, let us worship and bow down; Let us
> kneel before the Lord our Maker. (Psalm 95:6)

I worshipped God for the son He had given me. Tony left behind many precious gifts for me to cherish and remember—his smile, his wife and children, his love for his family, and his faith search for God's truth. My son would want me to know there's only one truth. We can get tossed to and fro with so many different ideas, doctrines, and theories, but we should stake our lives only on God's reliable, steadfast truth.

> And by faith he still speaks, even though he is dead.
> (Hebrews 11:4 (NIV))

The Lord showed me that all believers who have passed from this life speak to us with encouraging words that can help us with our faith journey. Our departed loved ones can give us incredible strength after they leave this world. It could have been something they searched for in their daily walks with God or what they valued. God made us unique, so their messages will be unique. Here's a list of some of those who have gone on before me and the messages they left me.

Millie, my mother in law—The future is amazing.

Shirley, my mother—Be strong in the Lord.

Michelle, a friend—Be generous to others.

Timmy, a friend in the nursing home—Carry the Word of God with you.

Lillian, my husband's aunt—Set your treasures in heaven.

Karen, my friend—All your needs are met in Him.

Tony, my son—There is only one truth.

Grandma Oleksak—God brings comfort to His children.

Grandma Long—He did not give us a spirit of fear.

Aunt Dorothy—Life is a blessing.

Uncle Lew—Smile at the future.

Babies, miscarriages—Every life is important to God.

Make your own list and see what God has done! Worship Him for those precious lives and for the truth they leave behind to encourage you.

7. David Ate

You can choose to live again. After a loved one dies, you can decide you don't want to go on without them. That feeling can manifest itself in many ways—lack of excitement, no desire to do things you enjoyed before, lack of creativity, depression, or in the most extreme case, thoughts of harming yourself. Seeking professional help is very wise if you have thoughts of depression or suicide.

Even after our loved ones are gone, God still has a wonderful future for us. In Jeremiah 29:11, the Lord told us, "For I know the thoughts that I think toward you, says the Lord, thoughts of peace and not of evil, to give you a future and a hope." But to partake in our wonderful future requires us to agree with God and His Word so we can smile again, hope again, and live again. We will feel so sad when we grieve, and we can try hard to keep our sadness under control, but at some point in our journey, we will sense God gently calling us to Him and release all our sadness into His Hands.

Here's a visual that helped me. Remember the arcade game Whack-a-Mole? The objective of the game was to hit "moles" that popped up out of holes randomly with a mallet as fast as you could. Eventually, as you continued to hit the moles, the game started going faster.

Picture yourself playing that game. You shift the mallet to the other hand when one gets tired. Then you switch back. After a while, your hands are too tired, so you use your feet. You get exhausted, but you keep going. You hear your name being called, but you still keep playing. Finally, after you have no strength left, you turn to see who's calling you. It's Jesus. His arms are out to you. He tells you to let go of the mallet and come to Him. You hesitate because you don't know if you can. You ask yourself, *What if those moles pop up again?* Yet your heart tells you to drop the mallet and run to Him.

With Jesus, you can find rest from trying to whack the moles, which represent the sadness you feel at random times, while the mallet represents your desire to subdue the sadness.

Even though it's a lot of emotional work to keep battling sadness, it can give us a sense of control over it. When sadness and grief pop up, we want to whack them back down. We hit at our grief until we're exhausted. We are battling it alone.

My fear was that my sadness would destroy me if I stopped hitting it. I was scared I wasn't strong enough to handle it. After a while, I knew no other answer but turning it over to Him. I saw His big hand, and I laid all my pain and sadness on it. I told God I wasn't strong enough but He was. I must have done that a thousand times until one day I found I wasn't scared of the sadness anymore. I was able to start to live without that fear.

God wants us to live again and abundantly. One of the verses that helped me was Deuteronomy 30:19.

> Therefore choose life, that both you and your descendants may live; that you may love the Lord your God, that you may obey His voice, and that you may cling to Him, for He is your life and length of days.

I remember saying this verse by faith. I chose life simply because I loved God, not because I felt like moving forward. Over time, I felt my heart changing until I really wanted to choose life. It was truly a miracle.

CHAPTER 6

My Family's Views of Our Loss

I asked my husband and children to write about Tony's death from their perspectives. This chapter is their view and feelings. Not all my children provided input; for some, it's still too overwhelmingly emotional for them to put into words.

My Husband Tony's Story

As I sit in front of our warm and comfortable fireplace nearly seven years after our son was killed in combat operations in Iraq, I find writing down how his death has affected me personally and spiritually is the hardest thing I've ever had to do.

While my dearest wife, Sharon, has been inspired and driven by God to tell her story with the hope of helping others, I realize I'm still emotionally wounded to the center of my soul and will remain that way for as long as God blesses me with life on earth.

Having your child, regardless of age, die before you is not just one of life's challenges; it's also not the natural order I believe we should find in a good Christian life. Nor is it something that gets any easier for me to comprehend as time passes. It's hard to put into words how many ways this tragic event has changed my view of the world in which we must live. But I can say with all confidence that my unyielding faith in God has become stronger than ever, and I pray my compassion for His people has grown exponentially as well. But it wasn't that way at first.

It was a lovely sunny spring day in Virginia, and pollen was thick in the air. I decided to take a very rare sick day off from work since my sinuses were flaring up. I was in our bedroom when one of the kids came in and told me there were some Air Force people at the front door. That wasn't normal. I thought they would be some of my military colleagues in the area working who had decided to stop in and see if I was home.

At the front door, I saw three individuals in class-A uniforms who weren't my compatriots. The senior member, a lieutenant colonel, began to speak. While I don't recall what he said, I noticed from their badges that the other two members were a medical officer and a chaplain. My comprehension of why they were there was immediate; I just didn't know which son they were here about; my four oldest boys were all in the Air Force. Sharon was in our little apartment attached to the garage, so I told one of the kids to get her immediately. When she came, the notification team performed their duties and told us Tony had been killed in Golden Hills, Iraq, less than twenty-four hours earlier.

Sharon sunk to the floor and let out a wail of grief. Somehow, I ended up sitting in one of the deck chairs. My immediate thoughts were for my daughter-in-law and our grandchildren. I asked if Angie had been notified and was told she had been. I was strangely relieved. I recall looking down at my sobbing wife as the children surrounded her. She cried out, "No! This can't be!" It was the first of many grief-stricken, surreal moments that would happen over the next few weeks, months, and years.

After an undeterminable amount of time, I escorted the notification team out. I began to contact our family. I know I called Angie to tell her we would be over soon; I just can't remember if I spoke to her or someone else at the house. I also know I nearly immediately called my brother Jim. Sobbing, I gave him the news and asked him to let our other siblings know. He said that he would and that he would come as soon as he could. I took a measure of solace in knowing he was coming.

Finally, I called my office. To this day, I'm not sure if I called my sons or if Sharon did. I also don't know when and how she notified her father and brothers; Tony was very close to Sharon's father and her brothers, particularly Paul and Mark, who lived in Florida. He would call them regularly whether he was home based or deployed. My son had developed a wonderful sense of family; it was something I highly admired in him.

It was then that I noticed a friend of one of my daughters was at the house. I remembered her father was also deployed. For some reason, I was fearful for her and was concerned that the events she had just witnessed might emotionally scar her. I told one of the older children to drive her home. I became overwhelmed with a new sense of mission. We had to get to Angie and the grandkids.

Sharon and I set off for Indian Head from Fredericksburg, about an hour and a half trip. I felt my head become clearer; I had a definitive mission to accomplish. While I had no idea what I needed to do or say, I was strangely calmed by the fact that we were doing something. I discussed how we needed to be emotionally strong for Angie and the grandkids, although even as I said it, I knew they were hollow words I was using to pass the time.

When we arrived at their housing on the naval base, one of the grandkids came up to us as we were walking to the apartment and said her daddy had been killed. We could tell she didn't know what that meant, but she understood there was much commotion over it. One of Tony's best friends and longtime colleague met me on the way in and told me he had been with the notification team when they told Angie. Tony and Frankie had arranged to have each other notified first if either was killed in action so their spouses would have someone familiar come with the notification team. It took me a few months to realize how compassionate that planning had been and how I was somehow ashamed of myself for not thinking of having the same thing done when I was on active duty. That little note was the beginning of a symphony of guilt I experienced over the next three to five years.

The next few weeks were a blur of emotions, time, and activity. As word of his death spread, we were overwhelmed by the outpouring of support and condolences that came to our home. One of my dear friends, Jon, was waiting for me as I came home the first day from Angie's with the grandkids in tow; Sharon stayed with Angie that first night. For the next three days, Jon showed up early in the morning and left late at night. He was a silent angel, there to assist in anything we needed—from running errands to cleaning to just sitting with me on the deck and saying nothing. It was a great comfort and kindness I'll never be able to repay.

When my brothers and sister arrived, they surrounded me in a cocoon of caring and peace. They ran the house and allowed Sharon and me to grieve without worrying about the logistics of feeding and caring for our children and guests. The support we received from our church, extended family, friends, work colleagues—some going back three decades—and friends of Tony and Angie still leaves me speechless.

At the time, I couldn't bring myself to talk much about Tony's death with most of the people who visited us or corresponded with us, an issue I still have quite often today. But just the fact that they reached out to us to express their condolences was a great comfort. In large part, it made us realize how blessed we were as a family, but it also demonstrated what a great, positive impact my son had had on many people from many walks of life. While the latter was a point that any parent would be proud of, it shortly became a main point in my questions to God about why.

The funeral and interment at Arlington National Cemetery were spectacular. Family, friends, colleagues of all manners, and strangers to Sharon and me attended; some had traveled thousands of miles to be there. Others attended on behalf of their sons and daughters who were on active duty and deployed to southwest Asia.

Our church was filled to capacity, an event I had never witnessed before. The service and testimonials of those who knew and loved Tony were touching and poignant. Even as I write this, recalling my son Jason's homage to his brother, whom he loved with all his heart, causes me to weep with sorrow and anguish.

My colleagues in federal, state, and local law enforcement provided an escort for us on the sixty-mile trip from Fredericksburg to Arlington, shutting down Interstates 95 and 395 to allow the over mile long funeral procession to proceed unfettered. At each entrance to the interstate, a law enforcement officer was standing outside a vehicle and saluting the hearse as it passed. I returned every salute with progressively more sobs.

As we transitioned from Interstate 95 to Interstate 395 for the final leg to Arlington, a twenty-motorcycle police escort led the way. At Arlington, I saw colleagues from the White House staff, childhood friends, captains of industry, military officers, family and friends from the farthest reaches of the United States, and Tony's brothers in arms who had been with him when he was killed.

Again, I never got—nor will I ever have—the opportunity to adequately express my gratitude to those who made my son's burial a memorial event for us, but I want them all to know our thanks is lifelong.

The company I was working for then recorded the event. Those who've seen the recording say it's tremendously moving and caring. After all this time, I still don't have the emotional fortitude to watch it. I'll forever be haunted by the sounds of the bagpipes playing "Amazing Grace," which has always been my favorite Christian song. Its mournful echoes across the solemn fields of Arlington, where my son is rightly interred with many of America's greatest heroes, was an honor his legacy includes.

My final note on the events leading up to the burial is about how grateful I am to our pastor, Ernest. I'm not a refined or cultured man. I grew up in New York, the son of a New York City cop. I spent many of my formative summers riding in my grandfather's and uncle's tractor trailers delivering heavy equipment to construction sites throughout metropolitan New York. My first real, full-time job was driving tractor trailers and working at major construction sites with dockworkers, carpenters, and teamsters. I'm loud, obnoxious, and vulgar when I get excited or upset. As we were going through all the arrangements this sorrowful and unexpected event entailed, I was often excited and upset; hence, I had quite a few not-so-nicely-worded moments with people whose only desire was to serve my family and me in our time of need. To those of you who were recipients of my immature and uncouth behavior— Ernest being at the top of the list—I sincerely ask your forgiveness. I still pray regularly that God blesses you for your patience and your compassion for me.

Regardless of the pain, sorrow, and grief we were going through, life—as it does and must—moved forward. Sharon and I were thrilled with Angie's decision to move to Fredericksburg to have her children know and grow up around their father's brothers and sisters. I had to get back to work. The kids had to get reengaged in school. Life was moving forward whether we wanted it to or not.

A little more than three months after the burial, our son James was getting married in California. Wanting to uplift the family spirits, I emptied a retirement account to pay for eleven of us to travel to Long Beach for a week to celebrate James's and Tish's wedding. It was a wonderful occasion, with the unique spin of having the wedding on a very large, paddle-driven "riverboat" on Long Beach harbor. The week was to be a joyful celebration of a new beginning, just what I thought we needed as we were still grappling with the reality of Tony's death.

For the most part, it was indeed fun and festive. Yet, as dusk was settling in and I was at the railing of the boat watching the twinkling lights of the harbor, I was filled with a sense of isolation and loneliness. Tony was supposed to have been in the wedding party with his five other brothers. I felt the first true pangs of despair and depression in my stomach; none of this was right if he wasn't there with us.

Yet life moved forward. In a matter of months, it was Christmas. Angie and the grandkids would celebrate the day with us. That time, I maxed out credit cards to make sure the gifts under the tree were legion. I wanted to hear the joyful peals of laughter and delight as kids and grandkids tore open their packages. I did hear that joyful laughter. But once again, despair and depression tugged at my heart and soul. It just wasn't right without my eldest son.

Move forward a few months, and it was Tony's birthday. We all went up to Arlington with balloons, flowers, and his favorite cupcakes. We neatly arranged the flowers and balloons, gave thanks to God for Tony's life and the time we'd had together, ate our cupcakes, and asked God to bless our families as we moved forward.

But on the way home, yet again, despair and depression descended on me. The day's activities weren't supposed to be held in a cemetery; we should have been celebrating with each other in person. The natural order had been changed forever, and I didn't know how to deal with it. That night, I cried out to God that if this was the way things were going to be from then on, I'd had enough and wanted out. If this was the consequence of trying to raise and lead a family in a manner that was in right standing with God and therefore be the recipient of God's blessing, I'd obviously messed things up so badly that my family was at risk of premature death as evidenced by Tony. I felt I had no right to lead the remainder of the family onward. If this was how it was going to be, I asked God to take me home then and there. I was convinced I had been at fault, and I didn't want to be a part of that any longer. But life—much to my chagrin I was still a part of it—moved forward.

Now I can see clearly I was a poster boy for all the symptoms of clinical depression. While I never had the urge to personally harm myself (and if you do, please seek professional medical help immediately), I lost all of what I would term my competitive edge. I still got up every day and went to work. I still paid the bills. Though

I had no interest in any future financial planning, I still maintained the house and property, but just barely, and I had no drive to do anything other than what was minimally required to keep us dry and warm and fed.

In the past, I'd meticulously cultivated and cared for my garden wherever we lived—a couple of tomato plants we grew on our stoop when assigned to and living in New York City or our forty-by-twenty-foot garden in our backyard in Georgia. I continued to plant my garden in the spring, but I barely put any effort into it beyond planting.

I stopped doing any type of woodworking, an avocation I had delight in before that. I gained weight, my health slowly deteriorated, but I didn't care. Our children married, moved in, moved out, got assigned around the world, bore us grandchildren, gave us great moments for celebration and thanksgiving, but still, I was nonplussed in my heart and mind.

I loved my family, but I was obsessed with the thought that my actions had somehow caused Tony's death. It seemed so obvious to me that I was unfit to lead my ever-growing family. I wanted God to take me right then. He was, after all, God, and He could provide a better way ahead for my family without me there to mess things up. But life, heedless of my requests to quit it, moved forward.

Let me give you some insight into my history and beliefs, which I pray are harmonious with the Word of God. Sharon and I were raised Catholic. I went to Catholic grade school, and she went to Catholic grade school and high school. The thought and presence of God in my life has always been there. Although it has been decades (mid- to late seventies) since we both found our spiritual path through the charismatic, evangelical, born-again movement, I have no great testimony to give you about a radical conversion. In fact, our most early teachers in the born-again movement were (besides my mother) Catholic nuns and priests in Valdosta, Georgia, when I was first stationed there.

No singularity caused me to turn away from the lifestyle we'd been living and reap the benefits of a personal relationship with Jesus, His Father, and the Holy Spirit. To me, it was a natural progression from a catechism background to seeking and finding spiritual and moral guidance through the Bible. God has been and will always be a presence in the core of my life; I can't recall a time when that hasn't been the case, but I have no great testimony to give on how much better off we are now in all aspects of our lives.

Don't let me mislead you either. I'd never been a choirboy immune to the ills and influences of the world. I had some lousy periods of time (aka sin) in my past when I opted to ignore God and take on the world by myself. Those times, however, consistently led to strife between Sharon and me, my loss of focus on what was important in life, and a feeling I was a lousy husband and father. I call them my "grey years." I chose to operate outside God's teachings and guidance, and I got what I should have known (and in my heart did know) was coming—strife, confusion, and sadness. I never had a time when I elected to not believe in God; my issues were my choices to ignore His Word. I chose to sin rather than flee from it.

So how am I not talking out of both sides of my mouth? How can I profess to have God at the core of my life but write that I spent four or five years trying to leave Him? I believe it was the eventual personal recognition that life in fact does move forward, and if my desire was not to be a part of it any longer, I was again choosing to ignore God. I was upset with God's way. I ignored the facts that my son's walk in life had been his own, that he was the one who had to answer for it to God, not me. I didn't want to acknowledge that I still had my own walk to be responsible for, not to flee from, because I was mad at God for allowing my oldest son to have been taken.

The Lord had the prophet Jeremiah write to the Israelites held captive in Babylon that His thoughts for them were founded in peace and that His plan for them included prosperity and hope

(Jeremiah 29:11). The Bible also tells us that our life will not be devoid of sorrow and tribulation even when we walk in the will of God (John 16:33) and that we should count it as something that brings us closer to Him and gives us hope rather than despair, depression, and anguish (Romans 5:2–4).

I'll say again that going through this process and recognizing it for what it's worth took about five years, and I feel that (and now know) I'm still recovering. I've come to recognize that true grief is a very personal issue. Each of us reacts differently to it based on our convictions and beliefs. Grief over the untimely loss of a loved one is not a weakness whose cause can be defined, identified, and corrected. My four oldest sons all went into the military and were all deployed multiple times to Iraq, Afghanistan, and surrounding Middle East countries plus many more. I didn't think I had deluded myself into believing nothing would ever happen to them.

What I did believe, however, was that since my wife and I had tried to raise our family to be practicing Christians who had personal relationships with Christ, that was a covering that would protect them from harm. When in my eyes that covering was shattered, the only person I had to blame initially was myself. I had obviously sinned greatly, I was sure, and had therefore passed the result down to my son, which in turn brought him out from under God's protection and made him vulnerable to an untimely death. Even as I write this, I recognize the false logic of my thinking, but that false logic and grief drove me to the edge of despair. But thank God, not over it.

So what's the bottom line? What healing advice can I give you? What solace can I provide to those in similar situations? Let me point out some things I can now see that helped me through the anguish of my seven-year walk. First, don't confuse grief with guilt. The loss of any loved one, particularly a child, causes grief and sorrow; those are natural human emotions that affect us all. Even Christ grieved and wept over the death of his friend Lazarus

(John 11), and He knew before He arrived at his tomb that He would resurrect him to demonstrate the great power and glory of God.

Grief is expected. Some of us handle it better than others do, while some of us need help managing the pain that accompanies grief. Time doesn't heal this wound. What time does do is allow us to slowly put grief in its proper place in our minds and hearts so we can move forward in life without the loss of our loved one being a constant, dominant presence in our minds. If grief is left unchecked, it can lead to despair and guilt. In my case, I let false guilt become a coequal of grief, and it brought despair into my life. Despair can bring only fear and death, and fear is the opposite of faith.

If you feel you're in a constant state of guilt, fear, and despair, seek help immediately. You must have faith in God even if you have to adopt a childlike faith that doesn't question why but dutifully submits to the knowledge that God is in control even when you feel the victim of a great injustice. Recognize and remember that God is omnipotent and omniscient. We Christians have elected to be part of His plan for salvation and redemption.

We will never comprehend some things about God and His ways, but God tells us that's in part because His thoughts and ways are higher than ours (Isaiah 55). Our faith can push us through our times of doubt and unbelief.

We all have our own walk with the Lord. As no two of us are the same, neither are our individual walks with God. While we might think we have some control over our loved ones' lives and walks, that's not true. While parents may be able to influence certain decisions their children make, the children will develop their own relationships with the Lord, and we must recognize that and support them.

I put that idea into context in my own travails by asking myself if the journeys through hardships I've faced are a result of my own doings or a result of my parents' or siblings' influence. That's now a rhetorical question for me. My life is the sum of my acceptance of Christ as my personal Lord and Savior and my submission to playing my part, no matter how great or small, in God's ultimate plan whether or not I'm aware of the outcome. I live my life with the knowledge that God knew me before I was in my mother's womb, that He has a plan for me, and that He unconditionally loves me with a love greater than what I feel for my children. I'll be united with my God and reunited with my loved ones because of the promises Christ made to us.

My son's walk was his own; my faith tells me that he played exactly the role God needed him to during his time on earth and that I should rejoice in the times I got to share with him.

Seek comfort in the Word of God. Take this book and the examples and experiences Sharon and the rest of my family have shared as a beacon that points to the Word of God, the Bible. Firmly ground your faith in the words of Christ. The Bible is God's instruction manual for us not only for eternal salvation but also for every situation we face on earth. Tomes have been written on the multitude of situations we will face in our lives and tell us we will find God's insight and instruction in the Bible. Ask your pastor for help, and look online for the many great, caring ministries that can also help direct you to the subject matter you need biblical guidance on.

Look to Job, who even after the loss of his entire family and fortune refused to curse God and die as his friends recommended he do; he went on to be blessed beyond all other men of his time because of his faith and belief in God. Look to David, whose eldest son rebelled against him and sought to kill him; David cried out with anguish and grief when his soldiers killed Absalom, and he mourned his death greatly. Yet because of his steadfast faith and repentance, David became the forefather of the earthly born Christ. The Bible gives us many other examples we can look to for comfort and instruction.

Who is in ultimate control of your life, you or God? If you answered yourself, I encourage you to seek professional counseling or medical help in dealing with the grief and mourning that accompanies the death of loved ones. If you answered God, seek His Word and guidance on how to handle your situation through your pastor and the Bible.

I cannot comprehend how atheistic or agnostic people can deal with the many ordeals we must face in life without a belief that we are part of a great plan designed by a wondrous and loving Creator who will walk with us daily if we let Him.

I leave you with the blessing God gave to Moses for Aaron to speak over the children of Israel.

> The Lord bless you and keep you; the Lord make His face shine upon you and be gracious to you; the Lord lift up His countenance upon you, and give you peace. So they shall put my name on the children of Israel, and I will bless them. (Numbers 6:24-27)

My fervent prayer is that God's name is on you as you deal with your grief and loss and that you know you are not alone.

My Son James's Story

People say that pain is only temporary. While that may be true, I think it tells only a portion of the story. Pain drives us to make decisions I believe have eternal implications. Often, the stronger the pain, the more we view the immediate and the less we can comprehend things further out or even eternal. When the dark of our lives seems most prevalent, the choice of faith becomes all the more profound.

The night of Tony's murder, I was excited to go to Bible study. My fiancée Letitia was on a temporary assignment in the States, and I was in Germany, flying for NATO. Growing up, I always looked up to my older brothers, and I grew to appreciate and love their roles in my life. I felt so strongly about their impact on me; it felt natural to want to share that love. So I began to teach and mentor high school students at the local international school with Military Communities Youth Ministry.

If you've never felt what it's like to use a spiritual gift, you need to. You feel excited and humbled as you realize your actions truly have little to do with the gift, that His grace has truly destroyed your sin, and, as long as you're willing, it will bring you real life. A life in which, when you speak what He wants you to speak, you will feel a power to change people. It could be one word or thousands, but the Spirit can use whatever He chooses, and it is amazing. I felt the Lord working this gifting in me as I drove to our friends, the Bittles, that night.

Our study was a small group of eight to ten high school students. We focused on Scripture and frying food. No joke—we fried everything and ate it. I promise that at the time, it was awesome.

As I finished teaching, we ended in prayer. My cell rang. I noticed it was my brother Mike. Mike and I grew up as best friends. Only a year and a half apart, he was the rock I could count on to always be on my side. I never doubted he would always be there for me, nor have I ever doubted his love. We have no problem being straightforward with each other.

"James?"

"Can I give you a call back? I'm at Bible study," I said.

"No."

That no struck a deep chord in me. Mike and I had done ministry through junior high, high school, and college. He knew the role a leader has, and the fact he would stop me sent a lump through my stomach. Though the next moments were in reality only thirty seconds, it seemed, and still does, an eternity.

"Tony is dead."

Some reading this have been through what I'm about to explain. I immediately rejected what he said as absurd. Although in reality it had happened hours before, in my mind, it was happening right then, and I had no time to let go of my hope.

"Are you sure? Are they sure he didn't just blow off a leg or some arms?"

"No. He is dead," he stated clearly. "He's not just hurt."

I can't quite remember the conversation we had after that. I think I remember asking if Mom knew and making some statements that I would be home soon. Honestly, it's my worst memory, and I don't enjoy recalling it. Even now, the anger pushes up against my soul, defines my thoughts, and drowns my surroundings in an inner monologue that's just a buzz. It was like that for weeks. Even now, small things will bring it to the surface. I'm not sure the shock of the situation will ever truly wear off. It just seems to get farther between fits. I turned to my group, still in shock, and told them plainly, "My brother was just killed in Iraq. I have to go home."

The statement hit me uncontrollably. I fell into a fit of sorrow and tears. People tried to comfort me, but I desperately wanted to be alone with my sorrow. I drove to Tish's house to feed her cat, George; to this day, I have no reason for why I did that. I remember screaming in my mind, *No!* Then louder. *No No No No No!* as I smashed my fists against the steering wheel, desperately trying to deafen my mental screams of sorrow.

As best I can remember, I screamed at God only once. I was twelve, and I told Him I didn't need Him. I think it was because my mom had banished salt from my diet because I'd built a salt mountain and was rolling a hard-boiled egg through it before each bite. I had no idea what blasphemy of the Holy Spirit was, but in my twelve-year-old logic, I had to have been close. I scared myself that I may have had to live without Him. I've never yelled at God again.

Later, as He healed my deepest pains and I learned what love was, I have never felt worthy enough to yell at God. Not even in the worst moments of my life am I worthy enough to question Him. As I contemplated this briefly, I felt something rise within me—a song. I had a choice, and I chose to sing it. "I love you Lord, and I lift my voice."

I'm not sure why this song was important, and to this day, I'm not sure I will academically understand the workings of the Spirit and what He was doing. However, it was a salve to my soul. It was the beginning of healing, the beginning of restoration, the beginning of choosing faith over pain. Tearfully, I sang the stanza again and again. I fed the cat and drove home. My youth group was waiting there for me. The young men stayed the night and helped me prepare to go home.

I tried to accompany Tony's body home, but I was denied that privilege because I didn't have the "training." My leadership profusely apologized, but it wasn't that big of a deal. Tony wasn't truly there anymore; he was with the Lord. His husk was important but not more so than knowing where he would spend eternity.

As I attempted to leave base and get on my flight, many people stopped and stated their heartfelt and sometimes not-so-heartfelt remorse. The honest "sorry" with a tearful hug was more important to me then the thirty-minute diatribe that was more about the individual speaking than my brother. My love for my fellow citizens built as President Lincoln's words at Gettysburg leaped out at me. My brother lived and died to protect this nation, and it is one of the best at showing gratitude. The heartfelt, individual, American military member is a treasure many other nations don't have, but the heartfelt American civilian who honors the military is the true strength of the military.

Three memories jumped out at me as I flew home. The first was about my father. From the story I heard, he had initially heard one of his sons had died and had thought it was me; that was because flying was inherently dangerous, and flying with NATO was no exception. As I got out of the car and walked to see him on the back porch, I was unprepared for what awaited me. My calm, methodical father was crying. His face told a story of immense sorrow and immense relief as his massive shoulders heaved as he sobbed. His depth of love for his sons broke every bit of composure I had left, and I wept for what seemed years.

The funeral was a blur. I opened the service with a worship song my brother Mike and I wrote. I'm sure it was confusing for some, but it spoke volumes to my heart. Looking back on that time, I see that it was the Holy Spirit holding us together as a family. Each of us made a renewed commitment to Christ; each built the other up; we refused to be defeated in any way. Christ didn't pay for defeat; He paid for victory, and we were going to live in that. No evil men, no sorrow, no sin was going to keep us from pursuing Him even more as we knew that was what Tony emulated and desired for us.

Hundreds of military showed up at the funeral, and I was grateful for each one. Police stopped traffic as we drove to Arlington. We laughed as we thought of Tony, who I was sure got a kick out of knowing his husk caused a three-hour traffic jam on I-95. As we put his husk into the ground, we wept bitterly. All twenty-one of the deafening shots pierced me. We watched as he was lowered, and as I paid my respects, I had my next haunting memory.

My cousin Paul, who was in the army, was standing in his uniform as we were passing by. We looked at each other, and I saw him truly, he with three black armbands, and me with one. We embraced. A shared sorrow and comfort was passed from one who had been there before. It was then I saw something that will live with me forever. In the corner, away from the masses, a three-star general stepped out of his motorcade with a flag. Clean cut, six foot tall, the epitome of military bearing. He strode toward a boy who was the exact opposite of the general—frumpy, unkempt, wearing a shirt that was too large. The general stopped, knelt, and handed a son his father's flag. I can tell you with no reservation that this haunts me today. If I can work just a bit more or prosecute my job in the military even an ounce better, I will do so if it means keeping more fathers' flags out of their sons' hands. We can crumble in pain and sorrow or live in some small way that honors those who fought and died for a country founded upon God-given rights of liberty and freedom. These are godly principles He still asks us to protect today.

I'm not perfect, but I strive to honor my brother. My family and I choose to let his life motivate us to love deeper. We worship when we are called to because we love Christ, who held us together during that time. We love each other for we have seen and loved those who gave their lives for ours. We strive to do all things as if we are doing them for Christ, because we know this is the way we can best honor our brother's memory. My oldest brother's legacy is one of victory, victory in Christ.

My Son Michael's Story

"It will get better, Mikey." I still remember the words my spiritual mentor offered minutes after I found out my brother and friend Tony had been killed. I had no way of understanding what that meant at the moment and what type of journey was ahead of me and my family.

The last time I saw my brother was at our home in Virginia. I had just returned from deployment in Balad, Iraq; I had taken two weeks off to visit my family. While I was there, I spent time with Tony. He was headed to the same location in a month, and the family gathered in Virginia to see him off. He made the usual statements while we sat around and joked, "It's going to be a dangerous one, Mike." He also made comments that this one was "different" somehow. Tony loved to joke and laugh, so I dismissed the majority of his comments as light-hearted conversation.

Tony and I had grown up close. He was one of the smartest people I've known, and he taught me many things. I learned my first scales from Tony as I sat next to him at the piano. He taught me how to play baseball and how to throw a punch. I looked up to him and tried to emulate him during my early years. Tony was always quick on his feet and ready for action. But beneath his bravado and jokes, I knew him as a tenderhearted brother who cared deeply for his family.

During our sending-off party, we joked and played around as usual. I enjoyed the time away from work and appreciated some much-needed downtime. During my deployment, several people from our wing were killed. One ceremony in particular stays with me; it was for a nineteen-year-old EOD tech killed in the line of duty. Our unit sat through the gut-wrenching ceremony in Iraq while leadership and teammates paid their last respects to a warrior who had left the world way too young. I remember thinking how much the young airman had given up; he had barely started his life but had willingly put it on the line for his country and his brothers and sisters in arms. I thought about my older brother.

One afternoon as we sat on the porch, I told Tony, "You better not be in one of those ceremonies." I couldn't stand the thought of sitting through a similar ceremony for someone such as my brother. Tony didn't comment. I expected something from my brother—some sort of reassuring comment—but he just looked at me.

That party in October was the last time I saw my brother. The week prior to Tony's death, I got a call from him at my office in Oklahoma. We chatted for a bit, and then I mentioned I had to get back to work. Tony's last words to me were, "Love you, bro."

A week later, his team had a ceremony for him in the spot I had sat six months prior.

I was in Virginia when I found out about Tony. I happened to be traveling to Langley Air Force Base and had just finished the first day of our weeklong trip. I had decided to sit by the hotel pool to relax. I called my mother to see what she was doing. After my mom's phone rang for a bit, my younger brother Joseph answered. I asked where she was. Joe hesitated. I remember him saying she was on the floor crying and someone in uniform was at the house. Even after receiving that information, I had a tough time comprehending what was happening. *Why is she crying? Was someone hurt?* I told my brother to give the phone to my father. I recall my father's voice being tight and punctuated. "It's Tony," he said. My mind still wasn't ready to accept what was happening. I asked, "Is he hurt or still alive?" For some reason, I refused to say the word *dead*. My father hesitated. I could sense he didn't want to say the word either. He finally said, "He's dead."

The reality hit me. It had actually happened. I was angry beyond measure. "How did they get him? He was too smart. There's no way they could have got him. Not Tony. He always came back unscathed. He was no stranger to difficult and dangerous situations, and he always returned home." I threw a chair by the poolside, angry at the men who had done this. Angry at my brother for letting it happen. I had told him not to die; I had told him I couldn't take that. I realized my dad was still on the phone with me listening to my ranting and yelling. "You okay?" he asked. I answered, "Yeah, I'm coming home. See you in a bit."

You're never prepared for the loss of a close friend or a family member; you're just walking down a hall and someone yanks the carpet out from under you. Amid the crying and surge of emotions, I kept asking myself, *What do I do now?* The only thing I could think was *I have to get home.* I told my boss I was renting a car to drive north to Fredericksburg. I called my pastor and spiritual mentor. I don't remember the conversation, but I had to tell someone. I desperately wanted to know what my next step was. *This can't be happening,* I thought. *How do I manage under the weight of this grief and sorrow? How am I supposed to exist like this?* The feeling of loss was unbearable. My head was reeling with all kinds of emotions and thoughts. Nothing immediately in front of me mattered. I recalled verses in the Bible talking about men not wanting food or wine. I finally seemed to understand the depth of those feelings.

When I came home, I greeted my family and stood in the kitchen while we ate fried chicken. The same thought kept coming up: *What do we do now?* Here I was, having a family reunion with my immediate and extended family and yet it was under the worst of circumstances. *Do we sit around and tear our clothes?* For some reason, I was at a loss as to how to grieve. My mother was crying, and my father was smoking on the back porch. People stopped in to offer condolences. For the most part, I sat in silence. It was too much to process. *This wasn't supposed to happen. Not our family. Not my brother.* I wanted to reach out to my parents and my family, but I had no idea how to do that. I felt that I couldn't take any more grief and that reaching out to another would make the weight too much to bear.

As we went through the ceremony, I felt I was being pulled through the motions. It was a whirlwind of hugs, tears, flags, and uniforms. My brothers and I were the pallbearers, and after the ceremony at our church, we lifted Tony's casket into the hearse. We followed the hearse to Arlington, where he was buried with full military honors. Family, friends, and coworkers paid their respects. Fellow EOD members took off their badges and laid them on his casket.

After the ceremony, my brother, Jason, and I stood in silence by Tony's casket. The finality of the event was palpable. It had happened. Tony was gone, and we were burying him. It seemed hard to imagine that his body was in there. It was hard to process the fact that we wouldn't see him again in this world.

After all the swirl, it took me a few days to process the events and everything that had happened. Many events will stay with me forever, but one in particular stands out. After we had loaded Tony's casket into the hearse, I looked into the sanctuary where over eight hundred people had attended Tony's ceremony. About half of them had driven the sixty miles north to Arlington to attend his burial. I was amazed.

As I talked with the people who had attended, I realized I wasn't the only one who had known and respected Tony. These people didn't just know Tony—they loved him. I knew Tony as a compassionate, caring person, but I was amazed at how many people he had impacted during his short life.

I listened to people talk about my brother. They highlighted so many of the positive attributes I had known he had. Tony had touched many lives during his time here. True, he was known as an experienced and intelligent EOD tech, but even more people knew him as a warm, caring, positive person—someone who truly cared about and loved others. I determined then that I wanted to be the same way; there was more to life than accomplishing great feats and achieving success. Tony proved that at his funeral. The positive impact a person can have on others' lives can be profound.

After the funeral, I returned to my job in Oklahoma. Again, I found myself asking the Lord, "What now?" During the ceremony, I felt pulled by the weight of the situation. Now I was home, back in my normal routine. It was then that my journey through my grief really started. I'd never lost a family member, and I had no clue what grieving was supposed to be like. Looking back, I can see the Holy Spirit was guiding me. I can see His gentle hand comforting and consoling me. Waves of grief would come and go, and yet I was never overwhelmed. I remembered the verse in James in which the Lord showed us He would never give us more than we could handle. The grieving seemed to flow, and at that time, I felt that was okay. I felt a release from the Lord to grieve, cry, remember, laugh, and process.

Interacting with my family was difficult during that time. My parents seemed to be grieving at their own pace. Tony's children worked through the event in their own ways. Some of my brothers and sisters seemed to ignore, accept, cry, and grieve at different paces. And yet somehow, all that seemed okay. During that time, the Holy Spirit showed me this was normal. Grieving isn't a formula; everyone is unique; everyone will work through the process in his or her own way. But the Holy Spirit would also show me there is a time to continue forward.

About a year after Tony was killed, I walked into my apartment. The Holy Spirit spoke to me as I threw my bag on the couch in my one-bedroom apartment. "You have to let Tony go." I got angry. *How can you say that, Lord? First, he's taken from our family, and now You're asking me to let him go in my heart?* I couldn't accept what He was trying to tell me. I resisted it. For a week, I tried to ignore that small voice. *That can't be the Lord. It doesn't make any sense. How could I give up someone I loved so much?*

After a week, something in me broke. I didn't want to, and everything within me resisted, but something told me I had to. I told the Lord, "I don't know what You're doing, and none of this makes sense, but I'm going to trust You here." I released my heart to the Holy Spirit and gave my brother to Him. I gave Him my grief, my memories, my feelings. I didn't know it then, but that was a big turning point in my journey.

Unfortunately, we can't always understand what direction to go when our hearts and minds are weighed down with the loss of a loved one. There is a time to grieve, but I learned there is also a time to get up.

As I went through the grieving process, I found it difficult to distinguish between my memories of Tony and the loss I felt. The only way I could move forward and heal was to give my brother up to the Lord. I had to give up the grief and the feelings. It was only then that I could heal and have healthy memories of my life with Tony.

I realized then that some of us never move from that phase. During the pain, it becomes very difficult to distinguish between the healthy memories of our loved ones and the immense loss we feel when they leave. The time is different for each of us, but there will come a time when we must release those feelings of grief, wash our faces, get up, and look to the Lord. Only then will we be able to heal.

Although the journey still continues, that day was a huge turning point for me. It does get better. You can live after a loss. The Lord will not give you more than you can handle, but we must follow His voice to walk the right path. The Holy Spirit will not force His way into our lives; if we choose to stay in grief and refuse to release our feelings of hurt and loss, He will let us. But if we're willing to trust Him even in the midst of uncertainty, we can heal. Not only will we be able to move forward, but we will also remember our loved ones the way the Lord intended.

My Daughter Rachel's Story

My oldest brother was a passionate man who lived his life to serve those around him. He fiercely protected and loved us and showed it with his actions. I remember a sweet memory of his thoughtfulness when he bought me a Disney tape I had obsessed about with his hard-earned cash from his first job. It was especially sweet since I tortured my family with my off-key voice and my made-up lyrics when I forgot the words to the songs. It filled me with joy when he gave me that gift. He gave a sly smile. "It's no big deal, Ray." That's one of many memories that sustain me when the waves of sorrow come. I am also comforted to know that he is no longer tortured by flashbacks and mental scars of war and injustice but is finally at peace with his Maker.

I was commuting to my parents' home on that April afternoon when I called to check in. My younger brother answered the phone with a quivering voice. "Something has happened to Tony. There are people here talking to Mom and Dad." Anguish flooded my heart; I knew Tony was no longer here on earth. As I hurried to my parents' home, the hymn "It is well with my soul" started playing over my car stereo. I felt peace instantly fill my heart; I knew I wasn't alone in this tragedy.

Nothing can prepare the heart to see your parents in full mourning. Mom was on the floor in an emotional puddle right where she had been when the Air Force notification team had given her the news about her firstborn. Dad was choking back deep sobs as he was calling to inform family members and colleagues about the news. Seeing how sorrow hit the members of my family was gut-wrenching, and tears flooded our eyes for days. Seeing my parents come together during their time of loss ministered to me deeply.

C. S. Lewis wrote, "When we lose one blessing, another is often most unexpectedly given in its place." Tony is sorely missed, but his legacy carries on. The outpouring of support and love I shared with those he left behind was beautiful and refreshed my heart. I remembered Isaiah 61:1–3: "The Spirit of the Lord God is on Me, because the Lord has anointed Me ... to provide for those who mourn in Zion; to give them a crown of beauty instead of ashes."

My Daughter Sarah's Story

I still remember where I was the day I learned Tony had been killed. It was around 1:30 p.m., and I was completing my MA internship. I had just finished my lunch break at the clinic. Soon after lunch, my phone went off. I saw my brother Jake's phone number. I thought something must have been very wrong if Jake was calling my phone when I was working. I told this to the nurse who was supervising and got permission to answer my cell in the break room. When Jake told me Tony had been killed in action, the only thing I could say was, "It can't be true. You must be joking. You are joking, right?"

I left the break room and asked the nurse practitioner on call that day if I could go home. I told her my brother had been killed in Iraq. I cried on her shoulder. I turned down a ride home. Somehow, I drove home.

I was in a fog. I went to work the next day. It's funny—the thought of asking for time off never came to mind. I told a coworker that my brother had been killed in action after she asked me if something bad had happened. She informed the day manager of my situation, and they sent me home for some rest. They wanted me to take time off to heal. Everything was just happening in a dream I was hoping I would wake from and find my family getting ready to welcome Tony home. I wanted him to fulfill his promise to teach me how to shoot a bow.

When the dreamlike feeling wore off, I became very angry with God. "Why did Tony have to die? He had five young kids and a wife who needed him!" It took a long time to stop feeling so angry with God. What changed how I felt was a song I heard during Sunday church worship. I don't remember what the song was, but it made me realize God doesn't leave us to grieve alone; He supports and heals us.

Healing from any wound takes time, time that is very hard to live through some days. There are songs, certain phrases, and other simple things that can make me cry. Some days, just holding my baby boy makes me sad thinking that my son will never know his uncle Tony.

Tony was a natural leader. I loved my big brother. We had fun growing up together. I can remember a few adventures that still make me smile. Some adventures became family traditions, like Capra Trivia and the games at Capra Christmas. But I do understand that he chose to be one of the many brave military men and women who stepped up and put themselves at risk to keep people safe at home and abroad. I am very proud of my brother.

My Son Joseph's Story

I remember praying with my brother Tony and the whole family right before he had been deployed. We held hands and prayed for his safety. I held his hand while we were praying. To my surprise, his clasp was firm; he believed everything Mom was praying for then. We never talked much about faith, but that moment said more to me than the times we had talked about it.

I was younger than Tony; he used to chase me around the yard and lasso me. There's a reason the Bible says Jesus is a friend who sticks closer to you than a brother. Brothers don't need to see each other a lot to love each other; their love is just there. We don't need to be constantly around each other, because we're always in each other's hearts. We don't need anything fake to maintain our love for each other; we have deep love and camaraderie for each other no matter what. We were knit in the same womb and had similar DNA in our cells. No one but God is closer than brothers are to each other.

I'll never forget many things my brother and I shared. Two in particular stand out. I was his ring bearer at his wedding, and I was also his gaming partner whenever I was able to get on the family computer. Those are just two of the events I hold in my heart; they help me feel close to my brother even today.

I saw the black Hummer pull up our driveway and three military people, all dressed up, come to our door. They asked to see my dad. I'll never forget the look on the older gentleman's face as I shut the door to get my father. I thought Dad had won some type of award. But looking back, I know why he looked at me with such regret and sorrow.

My dad brought them out back with my mom, and all my siblings started to gather. I looked through the glass doors. My mom was on her knees with her face in her hands. One of the men was kneeling next to her and trying to comfort her. My dad was in a chair looking down. I knew it was about Tony. I knew he had been killed.

I went to my room, and for the first time in my life, I mourned. I'd cried before but never mourned. I wept and said Tony's name over and over. Everything felt wrong. I called my older brother Mike and told him what had happened, and I did my best to hold in tears around my family, especially my mom. I wanted to be strong for them.

I never felt offended at the Lord for having let this happen. In fact, I never felt offended at the enemy either. I felt more broken than hurt, like a puzzle that was missing a piece or a tree that was missing its leaves. And it wasn't till later that the Lord truly comforted me through this dream. I was in Iraq with a platoon. They had just come back from a mission, but Tony was missing. One of the officers told me he got lost during the mission. After the dream, the Lord told me that Tony was on a mission and that He had him. I won't be able to see him again until later. He was lost to us but gained by the Lord.

I think part of my healing was that I needed to hear that from the Lord because I never fully believed he was dead. I didn't want too. I had to hear it from the Lord to restore my heart and trust in His plan. He reassured me Tony was in heaven with Him.

I still have a hard time believing it happened; part of me wants to believe he will come home one day. But I trust in the Lord and know I'll be the one coming home now and he'll be the one greeting me then.

My Daughter Danielle's Story

On the night of April 8, I had the worst nightmare of my life. It was a dream about my eldest brother, Tony. My dream was disorienting and confusing, but one thing was very apparent in the dream—my brother was dead. I woke up to the refreshing relief that it had all been a nightmare. My dream was about to become my most horrific reality.

I remember April 9 perfectly. It was beautiful and sunny afternoon. Some people arrived at the house dressed in uniforms. After talking to my father, he asked me to get Mom from the pool house. I skipped blissfully as I went, totally unaware of the devastating news those strangers were about to bring to my family.

My parents went out to the back porch alone with the strangers as my siblings and I watched through our glass doors. My heart dropped when I saw my mom fall to the ground weeping. Immediately, I realized what was happening. It was Tony. I remember praying and pleading to God that Tony had been only injured, not killed. Anything but dead.

After the people in uniform left, my father brought us all on the deck and told us, "Your brother Tony is dead." I fell to the floor and wept with my family. I knew what I was supposed to do right then and there—trust in God—but as I saw my family practically destroyed and sobbing, I didn't know if that was possible.

One of the worst parts was waking up the next morning and realizing my nightmare had come true. The first few months after my brother died were a blur, but the Lord carried my family the entire way. The pain of losing Tony was so real and crushing that it took my breath away. The pain hurt not only emotionally but spiritually and physically as well. Regardless of my doubts, every day, I begged and prayed that God would comfort my family, and He did.

Throughout the next few months, I did exactly what I was supposed to do. I went to church, read my Bible, and prayed to God. But despite all that, my heart wasn't healing because I wouldn't allow it to; something was hindering it. It took three years after Tony's death for me to realize what was really in my heart.

Within three years, my family lost Tony and my two grandmothers. One day, I couldn't take it anymore. I couldn't take seeing my family in pain and being torn apart. I couldn't handle the heaviness and despair in my heart. I screamed at God and asked why He was taking away everyone I loved. Suddenly, I saw the rage and the resentment I had toward Him. It had hardened my heart and had been building up for three years till the point that it had consumed my life. When my brother and grandmothers passed away, I prayed to God because I knew that was what the Bible said to do, but I was only going through the motions. I let my anger and grief be my comforts; they were my companions for all those years. I never trusted God; I never sought His grace because I chose my anger instead.

I never felt so alone. I felt empty, dead. I didn't recognize who I was anymore, and I didn't know who God was either. All I knew was the anger within me was fueling my every action. I wept for hours, crying out to God. I was tired of carrying this resentment. I was lonely and so sick of feeling empty. I repented for my bitterness against the Lord, and for the first time in a while, I asked for His forgiveness.

God hadn't taken away Tony, and He hadn't taken away my grandmas. He had never hurt my family or me. Instead, He was reaching out to us to comfort us in the way only He could. I didn't know how lost and hurt I was until I let go of my anger. Once I did, I was finally able to receive the peace and comfort I'd been longing for. The Lord couldn't heal my heart until I surrendered to Him and allowed Him to heal it.

Finally, I was no longer suffering. I was no longer lonely and empty. I was beginning to heal. The Lord found me even though I didn't want Him to; He accepted me even when I rejected Him; He loved me even when I hated Him. God saved a wretch like me, who didn't deserve it. Once I gave up my anger, His grace and mercy filled me and His love consumed me. I began to walk with God again. I wasn't just going through the motions of being a Christian as I used to; I was actually living as a follower of Christ. I used to be dead inside, but now I'm alive.

I will always have the pain of losing my brother in my heart, and I will always miss him, but I no longer suffer as I used to. As I grow in Christ, I continue to heal spiritually and emotionally. The Lord can break even the strongest of chains; and if you allow Him to do that, your life will never be the same.

I still struggle with my anger at times, but the grace and love of God are so much stronger than any stronghold. Every day, I have to make the decision to surrender to the Father and walk with Him, and sometimes that's not easy. However, unlike before, I now have the Lord to hold my hand every step of the way and guide me with His love and mercy until the day I meet Tony again at the gates of heaven.

> But God, who is rich in mercy, because of the great love with which he loved us, even when we were dead in our trespasses, made us alive together with Christ—by grace you have been saved. (Ephesians 2:4–5)

My Daughter Julia's Story

When I was growing up, I cried a lot. I cried about being yelled at by my dad or because my sisters didn't want to play with me, or siblings moving out—pretty much everything. I was made fun of many times. I rarely saw any of my siblings cry, and I always admired how they could be so strong.

That view was shaken the day my brother died. Watching my family weep over the loss of my brother Tony was probably the hardest thing I've ever gone through. I'm empathic; anytime someone cried or was sad, I felt the same, but seeing my family cry was worse. The hardest for me was seeing my dad cry. Up until then, I had always known my dad as a big, tough man who never cried about anything. I believed I would never see him cry no matter what happened. It tore me apart seeing someone so strong weep like that.

I have many memories of Tony when I was younger, but during the months after he passed away, I blocked them out. I remembered bits and pieces, but I didn't write things in a journal or do anything to document my thoughts during my grieving.

I do remember his funeral. We were all sitting in the front rows of our church listening to people talk about Tony and his life. The pastor told us to stand and sing a song. I saw so many people praising the Lord, but I couldn't comprehend how they could possibly be strong enough in that moment to be doing that. Everyone was singing around me while I was once again crying.

I thought crying was the only thing that helped my pain. I cried for hours, wondering why my brother had had to die. My sister Emily often yelled at me for crying so much. I was almost looked down upon because I cried. I often felt stupid because of that. Don't get me wrong; I hated and still hate crying in public, and seeing that my siblings were strong enough to compose themselves made me feel weak.

A year after Tony died, my siblings and I went to TAPS, the Tragedy Assistance Program for Survivors. Basically, you go away for a weekend and take part in many grieving activities. When I was there, I saw many people who had lost family members and could tell stories about them with a smile. Once again, I felt weak because I still cried about Tony when I talked about him. I learned since, though, that crying doesn't mean you're weak.

Just because I openly expressed my grief didn't mean I was weak. Everyone expresses his or her grief differently, and it shouldn't make anyone feel stupid or weak just because he or she is grieving differently than others. I know that I'm not weak and that my family isn't weak. If anything, going through this together made us stronger.

My Daughter Emily's Story

After my brother died, I received many comments from people such as, "Well, you really didn't know him that well" or "I know you hurt some, but imagine how [insert name here] hurt" and mostly, "Your siblings knew him better." As a very trusting nine-year-old at that time, such comments confused me. I'd often lie awake and wrap myself around the question, what is the measure of grief? I continued to think about that question for years.

I'm very grateful for my immaturity when I heard about my brother's death; that let me ignore most of the situations and suppress memories of the time. I was content in my denial. It wasn't until I was thirteen that I started to believe it and ache for his passing.

I was lying in bed when I started thinking about my sister Julia, who went through a phase during which she'd sob about missing a sibling. Usually, it was Michael, Rachel, or Tony. I would get so mad at her. I believed that only select people were allowed to miss people they loved. I'd yell at Julia to get over it; I called her a baby because she missed the people she loved. While I lay in bed that night restlessly thinking, I suddenly remembered my niece Tori. She and I are the same age; our birthdays are ten days apart.

During one lazy, summer afternoon, Tori and I were watching TV, and I saw her crying. I'd seen her cry before, so I didn't think anything of it. I just calmly asked her what was wrong. She told me she was crying for her aunt who had passed away from breast cancer. That confused me, because I was Tori's aunt and had never thought about her having any other aunts. I asked her who that person was. She told me she had never met her aunt; that was why she was crying. And just as I had done with Julia, I got furious. I believed she had no right to cry and mourn. I told her to stop crying because she had never even known the woman. Still, Tori cried because she regretted not having met her.

Then my mind brought me to the day my brother died, April 9, 2008. I was the last person at my house to find out about Tony's passing. It was the calm before the storm. I had been happily playing with our new kittens in the bathroom while the rest of my family was being torn to shreds. Once I left the bathroom, I saw my soon-to-be-sister-in-law Dillon and my brother Joe crying. My first thought was that they had broken off their engagement. My sisters were crying on the couch. I asked what had happened. Danielle said, "He's gone. Tony died." I thought they were joking. "That's not funny," I said. "Really, what happened?" My sisters pulled me to the couch and cried.

I realized they weren't joking. My thoughts went to Anna, Tony's youngest, and I cried because she would never know her father. At nights, I would cry because my mother had lost her son and my sister-in-law had lost her husband. I'd cry because I had seen everyone in my life I felt was strong die a little. To me, my brother wasn't dead, just somewhere off in the world. But that night, I was faced with a choice: either be in denial of my brother's death or face the grief and hurt from the loss.

For the first time, I cried because I had lost my brother. For me, that was the day he died. I also cried for my Grandma Capra and my Grandma Oleksak whom I also had never allowed myself to grieve for. I didn't stop crying until my body felt hollow and my eyes closed themselves. And that was the way I fell asleep for two years—with the help of tears.

For those two years, I felt hollow and numb, as if there were no bones inside me, only an ache, and I turned to other places to make the numbness go away. I grieved and mourned in secret. I still believed that I shouldn't allow myself to grieve, that I didn't measure up to the standards of those who were allowed to do that. I believed my grief was insufficient and unimportant because that's what I believed people were telling me. I let the hollow darkness swallow me because I felt unimportant.

That feeling persisted until my cousin Natalie moved to Virginia, and she taught me that I was strong and loved and was important to her and God. I realized the Lord cries with us and laughs with us. I wasn't alone after all. I found the answer to my question.

Of course I knew my brother, of course I loved my brother, of course I missed him every day, and of course I grieved. I feel as though God has called me to write to tell you that you're allowed to grieve for your father, son, cousin, friend—any loved one who you may have known more than anyone else or not. You are valid. Whether you grieve for yourself or your niece out of regret or loneliness, you're not alone. People can look down upon you for your age or the reason and the way you express your grief, but it's your decision to listen to them.

So what's the measure of grief? Who's allowed to grieve? There is no measure. There is no standard. You're allowed to grieve, and you get to decide how and when.

As a believer, you're not alone.

Tony and I visiting grandparents

Tony and his younger brother Jason

Tony and his five brothers

Tony fishing with his uncle Paul

Our family in Athens, Greece. (Top left) Jason, Anthony, Joe, Sharon, and Tony; (bottom left) Rachel, Sarah, James, and Michael.

Tony and Angie's wedding. (Top left) Danielle, Sharon, Joanna, Anthony, Angie, Tony, and Jason; (bottom left) Rachel, Joe, Sarah, Jake, James, and Michael.

Tony and Angie's children. (Top left) Tori and
Mark; (bottom left) Shawn, Anna, and Jared.

Tony in Balad, Iraq

All five brothers and family members carrying Tony's casket

Funeral procession traveling on I-95

Officer saluting the funeral procession

Our family at Arlington National Cemetery watching
Tony's casket proceed to the burial site.
(Top left) Sharon, Tori, Julia, Anna, Anthony, Danielle, Joanna,
Mark, and Angie; (bottom left) Emily, Jared, and Shawn.

Last family gathering with Tony. (Top left to bottom right) Rachel, Jacob, Tricia, Jason, Joe, Sarah, Mike, Angie, Anna, Anthony, Sharon, Tony, Emily, Joanna, Danielle, Katie, Mark, Jared, Julia, Tori, Kristin, and Shawn.

Family at Arlington for the first anniversary of Tony's going home

CHAPTER 7

Tony Capra—A Life Worth Remembering

This last chapter is for my grandchildren, Tony's children—Mark, Tori, Jared, Shawn, and Anna. It's a semibiographical tribute that highlights some of the most precious memories I have of their father. I pray that during the course of their lives, they will look on this whole endeavor and feel the love their father had for them, the impact he had on others, and the love his family felt for him. His short time on earth is truly a life worth remembering.

He was born at 1:38 a.m. on March 14, 1977. My husband was stationed at Lowry Air Force Base at the time, and I delivered Tony at Fitzsimmons Army Hospital in Denver, Colorado. We received congratulations and flowers and countless cards.

About a week after he was born, I held him in my arms and walked to a mirror. I stared at myself with this new little one and thought, *Wow! This is what a mother looks like!*

Jason was born sixteen months later while we were living in Valdosta, Georgia. Right away, Tony and Jason were very close not only in age but also in friendship. Tony called his brother Bubby, his name for "baby."

Tony amazed me. I would take him and his brother to the library each week and spend hours there attending story hour or reading books together. One day, when he was about three, we were driving home from the library. He asked me what the letters *c-a-t* meant. I told him cat, and then he asked what the letters *h-a-t* meant. I told him hat. He quickly progressed from identifying sounds and letters to sounding the words out in the children's books. I was astounded that he was reading at age three.

He was fascinated with planes. A family friend had a private pilot's license, and sometimes, we would fly with him. It was fun to watch Tony be so engrossed in flying. He wanted to fly one day too. He would check out books about planes, and I bought him toy planes for gifts all the time.

He enjoyed playing soldier, and many times when his dad came home from work, Tony would put on his battle dress uniform jacket and hat and march around the room. He always wanted me to purchase the plastic soldiers that come in a bag so he could line them up and march them around. His dad and I would laugh at how intense he looked playing with those soldiers, and I wondered if he would one day go into the military.

By the time he was four, he was playing soccer for our base children's sports league. It became his passion. He'd kick the ball around in the backyard and make Jason come out to play with him. During the games, I would stand on the sidelines and cheer him on. By then, Tony had a new brother, James, whom he liked to hold at halftime. But as soon as the game started, he grew serious and focused. He was constantly encouraging his teammates. I heard him many times tell a teammate to move to a certain spot to get the ball. Finally, the coach put him in as goalie. He seemed to enjoy that position the best.

As a family, we found going to church and learning about God's Word very important. So every Sunday, I would take him and his siblings to church. When he was five, Tony professed his belief in Jesus and prayed for God's salvation through Jesus Christ.

That was extremely important to me as a Christian mother, and I thanked God for my son. We heard about the program called Awana, Approved Workers Are Not Ashamed. It's still a Baptist-sponsored program similar to Boy and Girl Scouts. We all enjoyed incorporating Awana into our weekly family routine.

Until he was five, I tried to keep all unhealthy foods away from Tony. I made our bread, and there were no sweets of any kind. He'd never even tasted a cupcake or a brownie. One day, he attended the birthday party of a soccer friend. I dropped him off, planning on returning after I ran to the store for something or other. When I returned, I didn't see Tony with the other children. I asked the mom where Tony was, and she pointed to her kitchen table. There was my son eating a huge piece of cake. The mom laughed. "Your son hasn't left the table since he sat. He's eaten piece after piece of cake, and he even asked for more ice cream."

I cringed; I wanted to keep his little body away from all sweets. That day was a turning point for him. Now that he had tasted the amazing sweets, he was determined to eat as much junk food as he could. Even as an adult, he craved junk food!

We decided to get an Irish setter when we were at Francis E. Warren Air Force Base in Cheyenne, Wyoming. I thought a pet would be a good idea and could teach the children how to be responsible for a pet. When the dog was about seven or eight months old, I asked Tony to take him for a walk. Already, the dog was stronger than he was. After Tony had been gone for a while, I looked out the window and saw him holding onto the leash and the dog running fast and pulling him behind. He wasn't crying, but he sure was holding on and trying not to fall down or let go of the leash.

I ran out, stopped the dog, and took the leash from Tony. His hands were all red, and he had a cut on his palm from the dog pulling on the leash. It amazed me that he had held on to the leash instead of letting it go. He had a strong sense of duty even when it came to walking the dog.

While at Francis E. Warren AFB, I gave birth to James, Michael, and Rachel. Our house was quickly filling up, and Tony took the role of oldest sibling very seriously. The children got the chicken pox right before we left for California. What a mess! You can only imagine all the scratching, crying, and complaining. But Tony was determined to get back to the soccer field as soon as his pox dried up.

When Tony was about eight, I had the idea of starting him on the Suzuki violin program. We'd all pile in the van, and he and his brothers would take lessons in Lompoc, California. Their teacher was an older woman with a passion for the violin. Tony would work hard, and he did great in his performances. He would play the violin with Jason. Eventually, he was able to play quite a bit, but he never enjoyed practicing.

One Sunday, I took the family to church. At the time, I was very pregnant with my seventh child. After church, I decided to stop at a restaurant for lunch. Tony, who was twelve at the time, was sitting in the passenger's seat. He asked me what we were doing, and I told him I thought it was a good idea to stop for lunch. He kept telling me it wasn't a good idea, but I insisted on it.

At the restaurant, we piled out of the van and walked into the building. A young man came up and asked me if I knew where a cigarette machine was. I replied I didn't. He grabbed my purse and ran off. Tony ran after him. I screamed for someone to help me because I was concerned for my son's safety more than my purse. I couldn't leave his five siblings. The restaurant owner ran out the door to look for Tony. About ten minutes later, the owner and Tony entered the restaurant with my empty purse.

Before we left for my husband's next assignment, we sent Tony to Florida to visit my brother Paul and my parents. He thoroughly enjoyed himself. One day, Tony and his uncle Paul went fishing on a drift boat. Paul caught a beautiful kingfish. In a barter deal with a woman on the boat who had hooked a small sailfish, Tony got to reel it in. Tony worked for at least a half hour battling the fish.

The rest of the boat cheered and gave him advice, and eventually, he brought the fish into the boat. The first mate photographed the catch and then released the sailfish. It cost Paul his kingfish, but he and Tony agreed it was a great deal!

Our next move was to Athens, Greece. I had just given birth to our seventh, Joseph. Our biggest challenge was finding an apartment for the nine of us, not an easy task. We were blessed to find a two-story, brand-new apartment whose older owner was delighted to have children around. It was then that I decided I wanted to homeschool. My husband and I prayed about it and felt it was a right decision.

I was so thrilled about this new adventure and spent the entire summer planning. Finally, the first day of school was upon us. I woke up before the children did and placed a pencil, notebook, crayons, and a Bible in front of four places around the table. At that time, I had four school-aged children and three preschoolers. Even though I was already busy, I could barely wait until they woke up.

We had breakfast, and then we started off with a short devotion. We went to the dining room table. The three preschoolers were playing nearby. I thought, *What a wonderful day this will be!* I opened the large French doors that opened onto our wraparound porch. We noticed five Greek children gathered by the fence next to our apartment trying to peer into our dining room. Tony and Jason were making silly faces at them, and they all started to laugh. Laughter is the universal language!

There I was, trying to be a good, serious teacher, and my two oldest children were not taking it seriously. But I was tenacious. I cleared my throat and started again. I picked up a textbook as Tony was sending a message to Jason, and they laughed. Patiently, I started again with my beginning speech as their teacher. Out of the corner of my eye, I saw four-year-old Rachel falling into my sewing machine in the corner. She started to scream as blood poured out of her head. I knew she would need stitches. I told Tony to watch the younger children while I took Rachel to the ER on base.

As I started driving away, I looked into the apartment. I saw the dining room table set for homeschooling, a miniature classroom ready for all kinds of learning. But there was something missing—students! Not a child was sitting at the table doing work. They had all run away to find something to do besides school. I should have known then that this new homeschooling adventure would cost me time, effort, and tears. But I was confident this was what I had been called by God to do, so I pulled up my sleeves and continued with the task at hand.

After our many adventures in Greece, we moved to Valdosta, Georgia, where Jacob, our eighth child, was born. The house we bought had a two-car garage that had been converted into a big family room. It was carpeted and had plenty of room to use as a bedroom for the four oldest boys. I set up a schoolroom in the corner. One day, I decided to teach the boys about basic military training. Tony took the role of leading the troops. We dug foxholes in our backyard and ate MREs. It was fun to see my boys enjoying that.

Tony again went to visit my family in Florida. He spent much of his time playing golf with his uncle and grandpa. One day, Paul needed to finish some work, and he took Tony with him. He had purchased a new payroll software system that was still in the box. Paul told Tony he could open it up and try to install it. Paul never expected that Tony would figure it out, so he went about his work while Tony unwrapped the software.

Paul returned in forty-five minutes and found that Tony had the whole system installed. That impressed Paul. Tony teased Uncle Paul by writing a pretend payroll check for $1 million made out to Tony Capra. He asked, "Can you sign this, Uncle Paul? I made sure I took out all the right taxes."

During that visit, one of Paul's friends, an ex-navy sailor who had recently lost his wife, was very distraught. Tony put together a model of a navy ship and took it to him to cheer him up. When Tony gave him the model, he smiled for the first time in a long time.

The next military assignment we had was to Garden City, New York. We moved into a big, old colonial, the same style house we'd had at Francis E. Warren AFB. I loved the space we had. We could spread out even though we filled every corner with children, clothes, and schoolbooks. Tony and Jason had a bedroom downstairs off the kitchen until Tony decided he wanted a space of his own and moved into the basement. His dad and I thought it was a temporary move; he lasted six months before he realized it wasn't such a good idea. Danielle, our ninth, was born there, and when Tony held her for the first time, he smiled. He always enjoyed his siblings.

When our time in New York was over, we moved to Incirlik, Turkey. We enjoyed our time there; our family was engrossed in a totally different culture. Going to church was still a very important part of our life, and we got involved with church activities on base.

Because Turkey is a predominately Muslim country, we would hear the imam at the nearby mosque calling his fellow Muslims to prayer five times a day. We had a Turkish maid, Nafia, who made delicious food that Tony especially enjoyed.

I had no idea that Tony had met Angie, who was working at the NCO club on base. She was the daughter of an Air Force Staff Sergeant stationed at Incirlik. I found that out when he came running into the room where I was in labor with my tenth, Joanna. He confidently proclaimed he had met a wonderful young woman. Through my groans and pants of labor, I muttered that I was glad but that I was quite busy at the time.

I watched him walk out the room. I could see he wanted to marry this young woman. They did marry some months later in our backyard, which we decorated with Christmas lights. We invited all our friends we had met in Turkey. Nafia cooked Turkish food for the reception.

Tony and Angie had to return to the United States after the wedding because they could no longer be our military dependents once they married. They moved to California to live with my husband's brother, Doug, who had a nice home in Hanford,

California. Tony landed a job there soon after. Little Mark Anthony Capra was born while the couple were living in California. Tony called me when he was born. I heard his little cry. I wept. I was a grandma! I wanted to see my grandchild, but we were miles apart. It would be over a year before I saw him for the first time.

Almost a year later, I gave birth to my eleventh, Julia-Anne, and we received orders to go to Indian Head, Maryland. Prior to that assignment, Tony had enlisted in the Air Force and was being trained as an EOD technician soldier. He loved his new profession and was training in Indian Head in Maryland, so he was able to come for dinner and hang out with his family on weekends. Angie was living with her mom in Arizona until Tony graduated. During his EOD training, she and Mark came to see Tony. I was blessed to finally hold my grandchild.

At Christmas time that year, Angie and I found out we were both pregnant. Our babies were due within a couple of weeks. Mine would be my twelfth child, and hers would be my second grandchild. Tony graduated from the EOD school and returned to Angie and Mark.

In August, my daughter Emily and my granddaughter Victoria were born. My husband received orders to move to Korea, and Tony and Angie moved to Edwards Air Force Base in California.

Soon after, Tony and Angie moved to Lackland AFB in San Antonio, where Tori and Jared were born. Five years later, they moved to Eglin AFB in Florida, and Shawn was born in Pensacola, Florida. Three years later, Anna was born in Fort Walton Beach, Florida. They lived there for three years before moving back to Indian Head, Maryland. We were all delighted because we could see Tony and his family more often.

During his Air Force career, Tony served four tours in Iraq and Afghanistan and was awarded a Purple Heart, a Bronze Star, the Air Force Commendation Medal with one oak leaf cluster, the Air Force Achievement Medal, the Air Force Combat Action Medal with one oak leaf cluster, a Good Conduct Medal, and numerous others.

As long as we are apart, we will miss Tony. He was a member of a very large family and had brought us joy and laughter. He was a good husband, father, son, grandson, nephew, and brother to us. He was a soldier, a warrior, and a friend to many. But most of all, he was loved.

SCRIPTURES TO PRAY

(New American Standard)

These are some Scriptures that helped me during this trial. There are countless other Scriptures to help you during this time. At the bottom of the page, I included a prayer in which I used Scriptures to pray to God. Seeking Him through His Work will bring you solace, peace and a sustaining faith in our God.

- Matthew 5:4: Blessed are those who mourn, for they shall be comforted.
- 2 Corinthians 1:3–4: Blessed be the God and Father of our Lord Jesus Christ, the Father of mercies and God of all comfort; who comforts us in all our affliction so that we may be able to comfort those who are in any affliction with the comfort with which we ourselves are comforted by God.
- Psalm 46:1–2: God is our refuge and strength, a very present help in trouble.
- Psalm 34:18: The Lord is near the brokenhearted, and saves those who are crushed in spirit.
- Matthew 11:28: Come to Me, all who are weary and heavy-laden, and I will give you rest.
- Isaiah 61:2c: To comfort all who mourn.
- Isaiah 53:4: Surely He hath borne our griefs and carried our sorrows.

- 2 Samuel 22:7: In my distress I called upon the Lord and from His temple He heard my voice, and my cry for help came into His ears.
- Psalm 31:9: Be gracious to me, O LORD, for I am in distress; My eye is wasted away from grief, my soul and my body also.
- Psalm 62:8: Trust in Him at all times, O people; Pour out your heart before Him; God is a refuge of us.
- Psalm 23:4: Even though I walk through the valley of the shadow of death, I fear no evil for Thou art with me. Thy rod and Thy staff, they comfort me.
- Isaiah 41:10: Do not fear, for I am with you; Do not anxiously look about you, for I am your God. I will strengthen you, surely I will help you. Surely I will uphold you with My righteous right Hand.

Here is a prayer based on the Word of God:

Lord, Your Word says that if I call out to You, You will hear my voice and my cry for help.

I come to You, Jesus, weary and burdened. Please give me Your rest. Lord, You are faithful to all Your promises and loving toward all You have created.

Help me trust in You at this difficult time as I pour out my heart before You—the God who is my refuge.

Hear my cry, O God. From the ends of the earth I call You. I call as my heart grows faint; lead me to the rock that is higher than me. For You have been my refuge, a strong tower against the foe. Therefore, I do not lose heart.

Add your personal prayer(s) from your heart.

28481399R00106

Made in the USA
Middletown, DE
16 January 2016